Congrat
on your
with
So

The Book of
Wincanton

Roadside and Racecourse Town

RODNEY LEGG

First published in Great Britain in 2005

Copyright © 2005 Rodney Legg

> *Dedication*
> *For three generations of the Hiscock family – Freddie, Graham and Daniel*

All rights reserved. No part of this publication may be reproduced, stored in a retrieval system, or transmitted in any form, or by any means without the prior permission of the copyright holder.

British Library Cataloguing-in-Publication Data.
A CIP record for this title is available from the British Library.

ISBN 1 84114 410 X

HALSGROVE

Halsgrove House
Lower Moor Way
Tiverton, Devon EX16 6SS
Tel: 01884 243242
Fax: 01884 243325
Email: sales@halsgrove.com
Website: www.halsgrove.com

Title page photograph: *Scammell's furniture lorry providing a platform for the clowns at the coronation carnival for King George V and Queen Mary in June 1911.*

Printed and bound in Great Britain by CPI Bath.

Whilst every care has been taken to ensure the accuracy of the information contained in this book, the publisher disclaims responsibility for any mistakes which may have been inadvertently included.

Introduction

George Sweetman got here first, several times over, though I did not match his words to mine until April 2005 when I bought a copy of the author's 1903-dated study of *The History of Wincanton* from Queen Camel booksellers Steven Ferdinando and Di Hooley. I had already acquired his *Historical Pamphlets*. My draft manuscript was now ready to stand comparison.

The initial shock, amounting to plagiarism worthy of an honours degree, was that we had both begun by describing Windmill Hill man as the first Wincanton inhabitant. Sweetman rose in my estimation. Given that my entire format is chronological, I decided to leave Bronze Age man in his place, but it is unsettling to read your own words from a century earlier.

The second discovery was a delight. He had also debunked local folklore and fake-lore to reject legendary locations of the ambush of King James's troopers in the Glorious Revolution of 1688. Coming at the problem from different times and with totally unrelated batches of contemporary accounts, we had both come to the conclusion that it happened beside the track now known as Ireson Lane. Sweetman's choice of the site of Coylton Terrace pulls rank on my preference for somewhere closer to the Old George in the High Street above Carrington Way. That was the current eastern end of the town and the soldiers were approaching from Salisbury.

Thirdly it is a wise George Sweetman, marking the golden jubilee of Wincanton Temperance Society, who takes us back to his childhood when cottages were squalid and public houses plentiful:

There is in the minds of the aged a tendency to think more highly of the past than of the present, but it requires considerable courage, notwithstanding this, to maintain, with any seriousness, that the days of 1843 were better than those of 1893. Let us glance back.

He does just that. Despite having signed the pledge at the age of nine, Sweetman is obsessive in his documentation and lists his enemy's redoubts in loving detail, and offers a sting in the tail for the temperance pioneer who left Wincanton to run the tap-room bar in the Charing Cross Hotel. That I shall quote, because it is a neat story, but otherwise I will recycle Sweetman sparingly.

Following the example of the master and mentor I have concentrated on adding and amplifying his work. How well I have done can be judged from twentieth-century memories. Here I have had the freedom to range alone, following up incidents and information, and incorporating a photographic archive that is second to none. Wincanton files, fully stuffed, stretch from desk to door. I have written many other histories but this one begins at home.

All has come from the community itself. Since 1982 I have turned the National School in North Street into my word factory and a Victorian-style repository for discarded items of Somerset and Dorset history.

George Sweetman ended his main work with a chapter of humorous local snippets, so in that spirit I would like to round off this with one of mine, no less Irish than his choice of anecdote.

When my building in North Street was a printing works, for Wincanton Litho, our usage of the Greek word for 'stone' brought correspondence and a telephone call from a lady who addressed us as 'Wincanton Lifeboat'. It still has me chuckling as it spins around my head into the plot for a postwar Ealing comedy.

The cinema scenario is that a bureaucratic muddle caused the Royal National Lifeboat Institution to station a boat in an inland town that doesn't even have a lake. In my imaginary *Wincanton Lifeboat* script, Wincantonians take a pride in their brand-new boat and take it to Stourhead, where it is hidden in a Greek temple. The maroons go up for a bizarre midwinter 'shout' which has it carrying out a daring rescue to save boys and girls who ventured out on thin ice. The subsequent report to London results in well-earned bravery awards for the coxswain and crew. The problem is that they have to ensure that the admiral coming down for the ceremony thinks he is on the coast. Seagulls that were captured on litter bins in Weston-super-Mare are released from the bushes at strategic moments. It is no more absurd than the famous *Passport to Pimlico* or *The Titfield Thunderbolt* which was filmed up the line towards Bath.

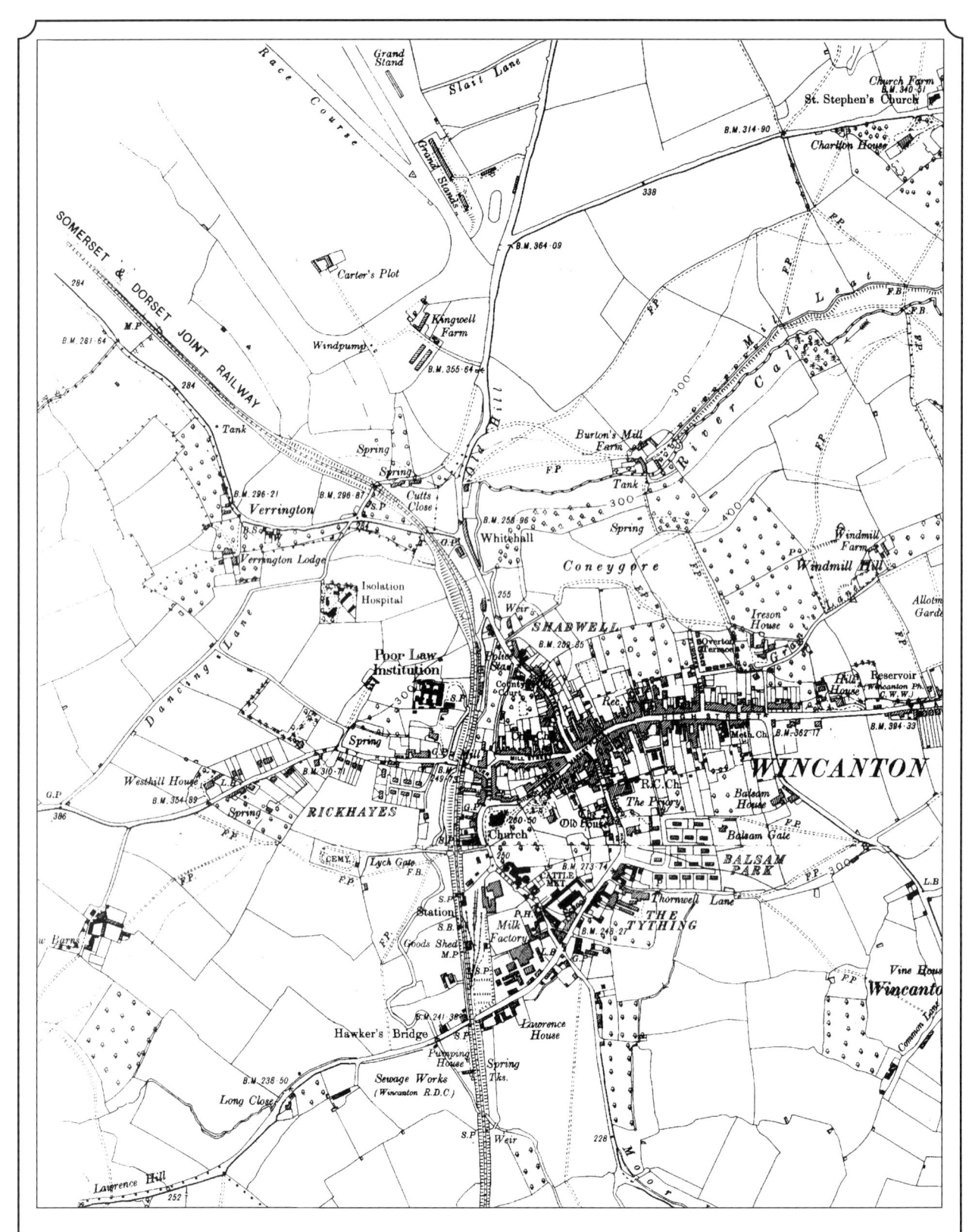

Wincanton as surveyed in 1884 and revised in 1929, from the Ordnance Survey's 1931 edition of the 6-inch scale map.

Contents

Introduction   3

Chapter One   Beginnings   7

Chapter Two   The Sixteenth and Seventeenth Centuries   15

Chapter Three   The Eighteenth Century   23

Chapter Four   The Nineteenth Century   39

Chapter Five   Shops and Trades   57

Chapter Six   Around Wincanton   73

Chapter Seven   Wartime Wincanton   101

Chapter Eight   Transport   121

Chapter Nine   Modern Wincanton   133

Subscribers   157

Further Titles   159

Above: *Wincanton chimney-sweep Tommy Jordan taking up his trade, c.1890.*

Right: *Young lady with gas mask and label arriving in Somerset in September 1939 when schoolchildren from Barking were sent to the National School in Wincanton.*

Site of the quarry (foreground) *on Windmill Hill, between Grant's Lane and Windmill Farm* (top right) *where a Bronze Age burial was discovered in 1870.*

The stone wall of Ireson House (top right) *and Grant's Lane which climbs towards Wincanton's earliest known ancient site.*

Left: Banners flank the memorials to the town's Messiter family in the parish church.

Below: A biker takes the corner from Station Road (right) *into Church Street* (left) *with the full frontage of the parish church being seen from Silver Street* (foreground).

Chapter One
Beginnings

Origins

As with the much more famous ancient place of Avebury, in Wiltshire, it is from Windmill Hill that our history begins. The name itself, in the centuries before mechanised wind farms, indicated the site of a medieval mill with windsails. What makes such spots so interesting is that in prehistory their flat-topped summits rose above the primeval forests, and provided nature's most conspicuous clearings, with viewpoints that gave early warning of changing weather and impending danger.

Wincanton's earliest known inhabitant, now in captivity at Somerset County Museum in Taunton, was found in a limestone quarry on Windmill Hill in 1870. Quarrymen broke into a Bronze Age stone cist which contained a contracted burial. The skeleton lay 7 feet below the ground. He had a brachycephalic skull – long-headed – and was accompanied by one of the largest beaker-shaped pots so far found in Britain. Beside it were pieces of stag antler, both tines and horn, and a flint scraper with an almost semicircular cutting edge.

The sides of the cist collapsed into the floor of the quarry which is now disused and filled. These finds have since been dated to about 2000BC in the Wessex Culture period which created the main monument at Stonehenge. The site on Windmill Hill, the location of which has been given as grid reference ST 718 289, is now a featureless point on the elevated plateau, being the field on the north side of Grant's Lane. It lies between a public path to the west and Windmill Farm to the east, to the south of an Ordnance Survey triangulation pillar (at 139 metres above sea level).

The beaker was a particularly timely find as the Honourable John Abercromby had begun scouring museums and gentlemen's cabinets containing country house collections for his exhaustive study on *Bronze Age Pottery of Great Britain and Ireland*. Published in 1912, in two volumes, it designated the Wincanton beaker as type A.3, with a close parallel coming from Culbone on the Exmoor coast. There a similar stone cist, also without any barrow mound, was excavated in 1896.

Apart from random finds of flints and pottery, lacking any archaeological context, Wincanton then disappears from the historical record until the discovery of a coin of Gaius Pius Esuvius Tetricus. The senator briefly ruled as self-proclaimed Roman Emperor, in Britain and Gaul, until defeated by Aurelian at Chalons in AD274. The place where the coin was found, recorded as 'Sutton', appears to have been between Suddon Farm and Suddon Grange.

Where Wincanton comes into English history is as a strategic location through which a tide of armed men walked and rode in the troubled times that found its first national leader. Alfred the Great (849–99), having retreated from Danish invaders into a stronghold retreat at Athelney in the Somerset Levels, regrouped at Egbert's Stone – otherwise known as Three Counties Stone – between Bourton and Stourton in Selwood Forest. From there, 'in the seventh week after Easter' in 878, to quote *The Anglo-Saxon Chronicle,* they marched to Westbury and beat the enemy at the Battle of Edington. King Guthram duly surrendered, both to Alfred and Christianity, being baptised at Aller, near Langport, and sealing the submission with a declaration of peace at Wedmore.

Wincanton, in Anglo-Saxon times, was named for a farm on the upper 'Wincawel' reach of the River Cale. This north-western tributary of the River Stour rises in Newpark Wood and Cockroad Wood at Penselwood.

Lectern, altar and stained glass at the east end of the parish church of St Peter and St Paul in Wincanton.

Allan Matthews from Rickhayes, exercising his lugger falcon, Jamie, beneath the church tower, in 2005.

The Cale joins the Stour on Marnhull Mead.

The parish is on the dividing line between two catchments. From land south of Wincanton Racecourse the water is heading for the English Channel at Christchurch Harbour. North of the town, however, it takes a different course and drains into the Bristol Channel in Bridgwater Bay. Most of Wincanton's drinking water comes from the Stourhead Valley at Penselwood, 3 miles north-east of the town, where Wessex Water inherited a maximum daily extraction rate of 2,100 cubic metres. Coming from the greensand – rather than chalk formations – the quality has the virtue of being described as 'soft', which is a rarity in the Wessex region.

Though I have already confidently given a derivation, to arrive at the origin of Wincanton as a placename is a thwart process, obscured by the mists of time. This has not prevented a succession of historians imagining they could see its roots clearly, from William Camden claiming that 'Cangton' derived from 'the seat of the Cangi' to Revd John Skinner who came up with a definition that can be paraphrased as 'the vineyard near where King Canute was defeated'. The 'Win' element – which was wine to Skinner – has been alternatively identified with 'a winding river' and a Welsh word for beautiful. It may be relevant that the highest point on Cranborne Chase, above Shaftesbury, is Win Green.

My alternative source, *The Oxford Dictionary of English Placenames*, gives a river name. Wincawel was recorded in 956 as the earliest name for the upper arm of the River Cale. Then the Domesday Book version, in 1086, is Wincaletone. This incorporates two logical elements, for a farm on the 'Win-Cale' river.

Since 1791, however, Revd John Collinson's version has held sway. It appeared in his otherwise authoritative county history and the attractive notion – it is no more than that – was repeated by local historian George Sweetman in the nineteenth century and by museum curator Puffy Bowden a century later. Sweetman retained some reservations but Bowden heartily endorsed Wincanton's reputation as 'the pleasant town on the Cale'.

There was no town at Wincanton when it was given its name. The mill and church, a farm and cottages, these were its lot. That, however, does not diminish the significance. The dedication of the parish church, to St Peter and St Paul, was the favourite choice of King Ine of the West Saxons who had been converted to Christianity by Aldhelm (640–709) who became the first Bishop of Sherborne. A medieval carving in the porch, known as the Donkey Stone, depicts St Eligius, the patron saint of blacksmiths, carrying out a miracle on a three-legged horse. It is a particularly appropriate sculpture, rediscovered by Victorian restorers, for a town with a racecourse.

Elsi was the last Anglo-Saxon thane to hold the manor of Wincanton (Wincaleton) in the reign of King Edward the Confessor. Then came the defeat of King Harold at the Battle of Hastings and the enthronement of William of Normandy in Westminster Abbey on Christmas Day in 1066.

The Middle Ages

Wincanton (as Wincaleton) was one of 34 manors given by William the Conqueror to his devoted henchman Walter de Dowai, and held on his behalf by Renware. The Domesday Book entry, in 1086, shows seven carucates of land – as much ground as

Evening sun brings out the detail of London architect J.D. Sedding's rebuilding of the porch, which in 1892 completed the reconstruction of the parish church in Victorian Gothic.

✦ BEGINNINGS ✦

Above left: *Heavily pollarded limes, in 2002, with a view from the north-west showing how Victorian additions* (centre) *have almost dwarfed the medieval church tower.*

Above: *Wincanton parish church, seen from the north-east, shortly before rebuilding in 1887–89 gave it a double roof-line which now almost obscures the tower from this point.*

Left: *Known as the 'Donkey Stone', this medieval carving in the church porch shows St Eligius – patron saint of blacksmiths – carrying out a miracle on a restless three-legged horse by shoeing its fourth leg* (left) *before reattaching this to the animal.*

Eighteenth-century print of Wincanton from the River Cale, looking north-eastwards from what is still public open space, across the track (centre) *that became Cemetery Lane in 1888.*

Holbrook House (centre), *its walled garden and stables* (left), *in an aerial view from the north-west in the 1960s.*

Left: *Hotel owners Geoffrey and Jimmie Taylor* (left) *welcoming Princess Marina of Kent and Madame A. Bascourt de Saint Quentin to Holbrook House on 9 April 1947.*

Higher Cuttlesham Farm belies its name, lying low in Wincanton's countryside between the Racecourse and Shepton Montague.

Croquet-lawn view of the south side of Holbrook House and its equally historic huge cedar tree (right).

BEGINNINGS

Geoffrey Taylor and second wife Joan at Holbrook House in the 1970s.

could be cultivated by a single oxen team in one year – with one of these, plus two servants, being held by the proprietor's own manor farm. The manor's Home Farm, operated as an in-hand carucate, had seven ploughs. Its workforce comprised 16 serfs, six borderers and five cottagers. As well as the arable land there were 50 acres of meadow and 50 acres of woodland. The total value was 70 shillings.

Holbrook House stands a mile west of Wincanton, just inside the next parish of Bratton Seymour, and was evolving from a farm into a gentleman's residence, rather than devolving from a medieval manor. The earliest known occupier of the ground was Gile or Giles Hose who in 1201 was a tenant of a hide of land at Holbrook. By 1242 his successor was Reginald Hose. In this 'Wycanton cum hameleto de Holebrook' the holders became Richard Lovel and William Husee.

The manor of Wincanton also passed to the Luvel or Lovell family of Castle Cary. Richard Luvel, the son of Henry Luvel, Baron of Cary, obtained a licence in 1263 for Augustinian 'Black Canons' to provide a chaplain for the Convent of Stavordale. This church appropriated Wincanton's tithes and was re-consecrated to St James, by John Stafford, Lord Bishop of Bath and Wells, in 1443. By the time of the Dissolution of the Monasteries, Stavordale Priory was attached to Taunton Abbey, when it was suppressed in 1538.

The manor descended through marriage from the Luvels into the Saint Maur family. Notable figures were Sir Richard St Maur in 1227, Lawrence de St Maur in 1283, and Nicholas de St Maur who died in 1362. In the next century, Sir William Zouche was created Lord Zouche and St Maur. The estate had been seized by the Crown by the time he died, in 1468, having left the estate in dower to his widow, Katharine, who died in 1472. The intended succession, to their son, John, Lord Zouche who fought with Richard III at the Battle of Bosworth, in August 1485, was also cut short by confiscation. He was convicted in 1485 of high treason for having aided the Earl of Richmond's insurrection. As a result, his Wincanton manor was confiscated, and reverted to the Crown.

Suddon, the manor lying immediately west of Wincanton, was held by Richard de Mucegros in 1227. Richard Chambermound was born there in 1345. It was then owned by the Zouche and Dibben families, followed by John Ewens senr who was granted arms in 1578 and died in 1585. He was succeeded by another four John Ewens, who take the story to the Civil War and beyond.

Walter of Wincanton was appointed parish priest at Claverton, near Bath, in 1403. He must have come from rich roots as he arranged the presentation of £100 'and other things' to Wells Cathedral, for which he was given the right to erect an altar on the north side of the Great Tower.

Holbrook, the next estate westwards from Suddon, was owned by Sir John Hussee in the long reign of Edward II, between 1327 and 1377, but the holder of real note was Sir Thomas Hungerford from 1381 until his death in 1398. He was the speaker of the House of Commons, and left his mark on another Somerset house, Farleigh Hungerford, near Bath, which he converted from a manor into a castle. Farleigh Castle became the principal home of the family but they still owned Holbrook in 1464 when Roger Hungerford and his son, Thomas, were beheaded during the Wars of the Roses. Robert's sole surviving child, Mary, became ward of William, Lord Hastings, and in 1480 married his guardian's son, Sir Edward Hastings. Their son, George, was a favourite of Henry VIII who created him Earl of Huntingdon in 1529.

Wincanton Mill was the subject of an ownership dispute in 1475. The High Court decided in favour of Henry Belknap and William Knoyle, gentlemen, and ordered the eviction of Richard Petyn and his wife, who were from Bruton.

After John, Lord Zouch, lost his Wincanton manor it was granted by Henry VII to Giles, Lord D'Aubeny in 1486. One of the King's privy councillors, he was

Hoteliers Geoffrey and Joan Taylor and the seventeenth-century dovecote at Holbrook House, in the 1980s.

Above: *The Blackmore Vale Hounds meeting at Holbrook House in the 1980s.*

Left: *Dating from the late-fifteenth century, Prior's House at No. 7 Church Street revealed a wealth of historic features when it was renovated in 2004.*

Scarfed and jointed timbers of the cruck roof of Prior's House in Church Street.

appointed Constable of Bristol, Master of the Mint, and Chamberlain of the Exchequer. Having moved westwards, to subdue rebels threatening Taunton, he was rewarded by elevation to Knight of the Garter and appointment as Constable of Bridgwater Castle.

Wincanton developed from a manorial farm into a market town. The market day was Wednesday. Fair days were at opposite ends of the agricultural year, on Easter Tuesday and at Michaelmas, which was celebrated on 29 September with goose as the traditional dish of the day. Visiting pedlars supplied tools and services. Butter and cheese were the main local produce. Stock movements in the spring – of prime breeding animals – contrasted with autumn herds of cattle and sheep destined for winter slaughter.

The settlement at Wincanton became the largest of a string of habitations built on and with the Cornbrash limestone that fringes the north-western extremity of the Blackmore Vale. The same geology is followed by the A357 road southwards to Stalbridge. Complications in the geological map, in the vicinity of Wincanton, include a fault line and a wedge of shelly Forest Marble in the dip between the old town and West Hill. The southern side of the town, including the former Unigate factory and Moor Lane, lies on the Oxford Clay. Having passed through the layer of Forest Marble, south from Hawker's Bridge and Southgate Road, the River Cale forms its own basin of alluvial silt.

An un-chartered borough with two constables and a tithingman administered the town alongside a far-flung court leet of Norton Ferris, near Warminster, which shared the Marquis of Anglesey as lord of the manor. Dowlas sail-cloth, linen bedding and silk-throwing were traditional textile manufactories which largely employed poorer females and their children.

The historic bridging points of the River Cale are below the Batch at the end of Silver Street, on the road towards West Hill and Castle Cary, and at Hawker's Bridge between Bennett's Mead and Aldermeads.

One of the oldest houses in the town, the Prior's House at No. 7 Church Street, originally stood alone on the southern side of the slope and dates from 1430. Its rear mullioned windows, spiral stone staircase and carved beams date from this time. The thatched half-house was then extended, upwards, into a two-storey gabled building with a tiled roof in 1580, with a fine cruck roof and an enormous Chilmark stone bressomer over the upstairs fireplace. All these features survive, plus a blocked window, propped by a Victorian cast-iron girder dating from the time when the historical fabric was concealed behind a bland frontage.

Jerome Dibben senr, a Roman Catholic, lived in Moorhayes Manor, Charlton Musgrove, and bought Suddon Farm, between Wincanton and Holbrook. The basic fabric of the area and its names were now established in the landscape.

Tudor two-light mullioned windows set in segmental arches at the turn of the stairs in Prior's House.

Curving staircase rising from the south-west corner of the main room in Prior's House.

Above: *The Dogs in South Street from the north-east.*

Right: *The Dogs takes its name from the Churchey family emblem which still looks out towards the back.*

Abergavenny Cottages, once owned by the Earl of Abergavenny, between Suddon and Holbrook House.

Chapter Two
The Sixteenth and Seventeenth Centuries

The Sixteenth Century

The most powerful man from the town in the sixteenth century was the judge Sir James Dyer (1512–82) of Roundhill Grange, between Shalford and Stoney Stoke. The son of Richard Dyer, he entered the Middle Temple and was called to the bar, in about 1537, rising to King's Sergeant with a knighthood in 1552. The following year, after election to Parliament for Cambridgeshire, he was chosen as Speaker of the House of Commons. By 1560 he held the top legal job in the land, as Lord Chief Justice, but had moved on from Somerset. He made his home in Great Staughton, Huntingdonshire; perhaps because it was a time for staying well clear of Wincanton.

The town's principal plague year was 1552 when the *Sudor Anglicus*, or 'sweating sickness' as it was otherwise known, recurred in epidemic proportions. It had been 'so dreadful' in London, between 1485 and 1500, that Henry VII and his court crossed the Channel to Calais. By the middle of the next century it was ravaging regional towns, with previously unaffected areas like Limerick succumbing in 1522, and Somerset suffered again in 'the fifth visitation' of the disease to England, in 1552. Death occurred in three hours. Some of the hasty burials in Wincanton, fully clothed and lying jumbled together along the western side of the parish church, were uncovered during extensions to the building in 1818.

The Wincanton Charter was granted on 17 March 1556 by Mary Tudor, for two fairs annually, and a market each fortnight, to be held every other Wednesday.

Henry Hastings, 3rd Earl of Huntingdon, sold his Holbrook property to John Farewell of Bishops Hull, near Taunton, in the second half of the sixteenth century. The precise date is uncertain, but by 1558 Simon Farewell and his wife Dorothy were living at Holbrook. Dorothy was the daughter of Richard Dyer of Bratton St Mary and the estate was bought 'so that she wouldn't have to live too far from her old home.'

Wincanton-born Dr George Croyden (1514–78) went to Westminster School and achieved his doctorate in divinity. From London he went to Oxford, and there he stayed, rising through the collegiate ranks from student to censor and as canon to treasurer. His monument is on a column in Oxford Cathedral. Wincanton has its mention in the Latin inscription. George Croyden owned 32 acres at Charlton Musgrove where 'Croyden Park' outlived him as a placename for three centuries.

The home of Jerome Dibben junr, at Moorhayes Manor was raided in 1583 when magistrates and the militia relieved him of Catholic books and tracts as nerves became frayed ahead of the Spanish Armada, in 1588.

Springs at Thornwell and Shatterwell Shoots have been known under their present names since 1558,

Above and right: The Dogs, seen from the south-east, provided the midway stop for the Prince of Orange – between Brixham and Westminster – in the Glorious Revolution of 1688.

The east entrance to the Dogs, facing South Street, appropriately boasting a 'Beware of the Dog' sign.

although both have much older origins. Rachael's Pond, above Thornwell, is said to take its name from a woman who drowned herself there.

Medieval Wincanton was growing up around a series of wells or cisterns. These still exist, although now usually capped by concrete, underneath later buildings such as those around the Market Place. Here in the winter of 1991–92 I explored culverts and overflow passages beneath the Georgian house on the north-west side. These wells and associated box-drains are known in the town as 'the tunnels'.

The main well is set beside and under the pavement of North Street and is the size of an average bathroom. Its sides are corbelled with circular stonework that widens as it deepens. It seems to have been fed from an inner well that owner Stephen Broughton discovered beneath the centre of his building in 1988. Although this is only about 5 feet deep it appears to surround a spring.

The two wells were linked by a water channel and other tunnels, which were dry, lead off both under the building and the road. These are so extensive that they must pre-date the building and are also out of scale with what would have been needed for domestic water consumption. I came to the conclusion that they must have been the reservoir for the town's water-supply as the public pump was located nearby in the Market Place. Roger Richards, writing in *The Visitor*, agreed with my findings:

He was almost certainly right. Early in the eighteenth-century, Wincanton's market trustees maintained a conduit in the Market Place which was supplied by water from Bayford Hill. In 1740 they agreed to rent a supply from a new well but this turned out to be inadequate, so in 1742 they decided to build a reservoir which served the town until 1874 when water was piped in from Penselwood. In the absence of evidence of any other reservoir in the vicinity of the pump, the large well beneath Mr Broughton's building must surely have been that reservoir. And if that is the case, it suggests that rebuilding of the White Hart following the fire of 1707 took place after 1742.

My original report in 1992 of crawling into these damp and dark holes spurred ex-Mill Street resident Karen Wike into contacting *The Visitor* magazine from Bristol:

There were many legends of such tunnels and Puffy Bowden used to say that they had been built so that people could escape persecution. Looking at the pictures, however, they seem a bit elaborate for that, with brick walling, and without an extension lead or a torch one would soon drop down into a sump or cistern. I suppose they would have had tallow candles but they wouldn't have been of any use if one's passage was blocked by a wall.

David Gates also wrote, from Bookham, near Leatherhead, Surrey:

In the cellar of Tout Hill House, where I lived with my parents, Mr and Mrs Stanley Gates, there is a water-hole containing absolutely clear water, the level of which never varied. It must have been in the early 1940s that I last saw it but, as I recall, the hole was about 18 inches across. I think a stone slab covered the hole.

Ruth Keynes told us that a Tunnels Working Party had been formed in 1982 and mapped the network as recorded by Mr Gray, a retired sanitary inspector:

The cellars beneath what was originally the Greyhound were extremely interesting. Here a tunnel, approximately 3 metres below pavement level, passed under the road in the direction of the constituency Conservative headquarters. This was cleared of debris for a length of 3.5 metres when it became collapsed, making it impossible to proceed further. It was constructed of regular stone, coursing with an arched roof, 1.7 metres high and 0.4 metres wide, similar to some of the earlier tunnels in Exeter.

Dr Ian Burrow, the county archaeologist, probed culverts beneath the lawn of Balsam House at the invitation of Colonel Holder in August 1983. They had appeared during the drought that year as lines of scorched grass. These, however, he deemed to be no earlier than the colonel's Jacobean home, and a further survey with resistivity meters, towards the

THE SIXTEENTH & SEVENTEENTH CENTURIES

Abergavenny Cottages from the east.

Left: *Rustic remains of a corrugated-iron shed in a small wood at Abergavenny.*

Below: *The road at Abergavenny was the turnpike route from Wincanton to Castle Cary and Bristol.*

Foot-and-mouth disease signs and disinfectant dip at Suddon Grange Farm in 2001.

Dogs, failed to find a further series of tunnels. Current opinion is that they are confined to the ancient main streets of the town, with access points beside their original buildings, and provided the town's drinking-water. Culverts took the overflow, to deal with too much of a good thing during flash floods, down to the River Cale which acted as an open drain.

In the Castle Cary direction, Suddon Elm stood at the junction of Dancing Lane with the road across West Hill, and is mentioned in documents of 1539 and 1651. Another big elm stood beside Balsam House, and was the 'last huge tree in the town' – being 17 feet in girth – until its demise in the twentieth century.

The Seventeenth Century

The ecclesiastical *Visitation of Somerset* from 1623 lists the following well-heeled inhabitants from in and around Wincanton:

John Ewens senr of Suddon
John Ewens junr (aged 18) of Suddon
James Farewell of Holbrook
John Glyn
Lawrence Glyn
Robert Huson
Barnaby Lewis
Humphrey Newman
Roger Newman of Charlton Musgrove
William Plympton
William Stroud
William Swanton

Of these, and their successors, six local gentlemen were fined – under a process called 'compounding' – for failing to attend the coronation of King Charles I in 1623. Their respective ill-fated forfeits give an indication of relative wealth:

Andrew Ewens of Penselwood (£10)
John Ewens of Suddon (£10)
James Farewell of Holbrook (£25)
Barnaby Lewis (£10)
Humphrey Newman (£14)
William Swanton (£10)

Seven people from Wincanton sailed on *The Angel Gabriel* from Bristol to North America in 1631. This 240-ton vessel, which carried 16 guns, was wrecked by the 'Great Gale' at Pemaquid Harbour in 1635. She supplied settlers to Sir Ferdinando Gorges, a stalwart Royalist, who held a wide tract of New Somerset.

They were joined in the summer of 1638 by William Dyer from Bratton Seymour, his wife Mary Longe from Wincanton, and 16 others from Wincanton. William Dyer is credited with having founded the settlement of Portsmouth, Rhode Island, and they also had pioneering connections with Newport.

The third John Ewens to own Suddon Grange had four sons who in 1623 were named as John (18), Edward (14), Maurice (12) and Matthew (9). George Sweetman, in his *History of Wincanton* followed their fortunes:

This John, in 1653, was described as a 'Convict Papist' and was sequestered by the Parliamentary party, and went to Stavordale to live. In 1672 he is described on the register of the College of Heralds as of Suddon, and 67 years of age. His brother Maurice was a notable character, and will be referred to again. It may be well to remark here that the name of Evans and Ewens appear to have been used interchangeably.

As the Civil War ebbed towards its finale, Lord Goring – the King's Commander in Somerset – was marching from Yeovil to Bruton on 1 April 1645. He heard that a detachment of 'Parliamentary horse and foot' were 5 miles away at Wincanton. Goring sent Major-General John Digby to investigate, with 1,200 Royalist horsemen and dragoons. They swept through the town but found only one officer and 12 men who were taken prisoner.

Digby then heard that 'others were quartered in some three or four villages near about two miles off' and 'fell in upon them' with overwhelming force. A total of 100 prisoners, 300 horses, and 100 pistols and muskets were captured, mainly from the regiments of Colonel Popham and Colonel Morley, 'and with them two colours or cornets of horse, one being Master Wansey's'. The latter carried the following motto: 'For lawful laws and liberties.'

This contemporary account, the *Mercurius Aulicus* in the British Library, records that the Royalist forces returned to Bruton at nightfall. Their supremacy was short-lived, however, as the King's men were routed at the Battle of Langport, on 10 July 1645, after which Parliament reigned in the West of England. The Royalist cause ended on the scaffold with the execution of King Charles I in 1649.

The 'Mancon Howse' (Mansion House) on Tout Hill was sold by James Churchey on 25 February 1651 to Barnaby Baker from the Close in Salisbury. He also parted with 400 acres of land, westwards from Wincanton to Maperton, where Anne Churchey, daughter of Thomas Churchey, married Thomas Strode of Maperton House. The remaining Churcheys in Wincanton moved from their other home, Temple Court in South Street, to establish a new manor-house which became known as the Dogs. Barnaby Lewis was living in Balsam House which was another of the town's mansions.

Money was in short supply, literally, because of the upheavals of these troubled times. Traders therefore issued their own small change. Token coins issued in the town carry the names of William Ivy at the Seven Stars in 1659 and Benjamin Lewis at the Black Lion in 1667.

Hugh Jones from Wincanton, who sailed to Massachusetts from Weymouth in 1652, settled in Naumkeag, which the colonists renamed as Salem. Jones had been accompanied by Captain David Meade, also from Wincanton, who led a cavalry unit in Oliver Cromwell's New Model Army. Hugh Jones married Hannah Tompkins on 26 June 1660. She died on 10 May 1672 and he then married Mary Foster.

Herodias Longe, Mary Dyer's sister from Wincanton, led an eventful life across the Atlantic. Having been a child bride in London to John Hicks, who deserted her in New England, she married George Gardiner who was from Wincanton. That marriage also failed and her third and final steps down the aisle, in 1665, were with John Porter. He seems to have been related to Puritan preacher 'Deliverance' Porter.

The sermons of Revd John Sacheverell junr, the rector of Wincanton, were likened by his parishioners to an overdose of medicine that did not agree with them. He was burnt in effigy on Bayford Hill to mark the Restoration of King Charles II, on 29 May 1660, and was ejected from his position in 1662, as were his Nonconformist brothers, Timothy and Philologus. They were the sons of Revd John Sacheverell senr of East Stoke and Langton Matravers in the Isle of Purbeck, who died in 1651 at the high point of Oliver Cromwell's Commonwealth.

The backlash against Puritanism, following the Restoration, was being pursued in earnest. Divine intervention was suspected as the world shook and shuddered to earthquakes and global cooling. Famines and frosts gripped the land in a vice of biblical proportions. The wrath of God was seen behind such calamities and communities across the northern hemisphere looked for scapegoats. 'Thou shalt not suffer a witch to live,' was an answer plucked from the Bible.

Depositions relating to the witchcraft trials of the seventeenth century include the following 'confession' signed by Elizabeth Style from Wincanton. It was dictated to lawyer Robert Hunt in 1664:

The Devil about ten years since appeared to me in the garb of a handsome man, and afterwards in the shape of a black dog. He promised me money and a long life, on the conditions of signing a bond with my blood, and handing my soul over to him, and permitting him to suck my blood when he desired it. This I granted him after four solicitations, upon which he pricked the fourth finger of my right hand, between the middle and upper joint.

For this favour the Devil gave sixpence, and vanished with the paper. And ever after he often appeared to me in the shape of a man, dog, cat or fly. When I desired to hurt anyone I called the spirit by the name of Robin and invoked him in the following manner: 'O, Satan, give me my purpose.'

About a month before this trial I desired to harm Elizabeth Hall, and to thrust thorns into her flesh, so accordingly a meeting was held on the common [Leigh Common] *near Trister Gate, where I met Alice Duke, Ann Bishop and Mary Penny. Alice Duke had brought a picture in wax, which was intended for* [to represent] *Elizabeth Hall, to be baptised by Satan, who appeared in black clothes and performed the ceremony by anointing the effigy with oil, saying: 'I baptise thee with oil, etc.'*

Then this figure was struck through with thorns by all present. After which, we had wine, cakes, and roast meat provided by the gentleman in black. When I wished to injure man or beast, I made an image of the person or animal in wax, which must then be baptised by the Devil, for even our power is limited by the will of the matter.

Elizabeth Style stood trial in Taunton and was sentenced to burn. Mercifully, before the date set for the execution, she died in prison at Taunton Castle.

The roadside triangle of grass where Beech Lane joined the main road at the eastern end of Leigh Common became known as Witches Corner. It has been confused, however, with the site of a medieval Mizmaze at Leigh near Sherborne. The cause of mix-up was Joseph Glanvill whose *Sadducimus Triumphatus*, published in 1681, mentions both the Leigh Common, Somerset, case and that of what we would call poltergeist activity at Leigh in Dorset. Joseph Glanvill, who with Henry More was among the first psychic researchers, says of Alice Duke that 'she had been at several meetings in Lie [how it is pronounced] Common, and other places in the night'. As Alice was a Wincanton lady, there can hardly be any doubt about the primary location, though in Olive Knott's *Witches of Dorset* her broomstick takes her yet further afield, to another Leigh Common on the other side of Wimborne.

Ironically, what the Nonconformists escaped from on this side of the Atlantic Ocean they proceeded to inflict upon each other on arrival in the New World.

They brought their own demons which were released in an orgy of internecine persecution that culminated in witchcraft hysteria at Salem.

Mary Dyer, a Quaker from Wincanton, fell foul of repression. She followed Anne Hutchinson to Rhode Island, in 1637, and returned to England in 1650. On going back across the Atlantic in 1657 her activities in Boston infuriated the authorities. After being arrested and banished from the town she returned twice to comfort imprisoned Quakers in 1659 and 1660. This enraged her opponents. She was condemned for sedition and hanged from a tree. Mary was the sister of the thrice-married Herodias Dyer.

Revd Robert Gutch, from Wincanton, was the first settler in what became the community of Bath, Maine, in 1665. Edward Ewens senr (1607–67), from Suddon at Wincanton, died in Exeter, New Somerset. In 1668 his son, Edward Ewens junr, joined the Freke family in Boston. The two were already linked as John Freke (died 1674) had married Katherine Ewens. Edward married a Miss Clarke in Boston.

Puritan soldier John Langley left Wincanton for Ireland in 1651 and was wounded in the siege of Clonmell. On 3 March 1674 he wrote his will, a copy of which found its way to historian George Sweetman:

I do leave all my house, goods and farm of Black Kittle of 253 acres to my son, commonly called Stubborn Jack to him and his heirs for ever, provided he marries a Protestant woman, but not Alice Kendrick who called me Oliver [Cromwell]'s whelp. My new buckskin breeches, and my silver tobacco stopper with J.L. on the top I give to Richard Richards, my comrade, who helped me off at the storming of Clonmell, when I was shot through the leg.

My son John shall keep my body above ground six days and six nights after I am dead, and Grace Kendrick shall lay me out, who shall have for doing so five shillings. My body shall be put upon the oak table in the brown room, and 50 Irishmen shall be invited to my wake, and every one shall have two quarts of the best acque vite, and each one a skereen dish and knife laid before him and when the liquor is out, nail up my coffin and commit me to the earth whence I came. This is my will.

Maurice Ewens (1611–87), brother of Edward from Suddon, also made his mark far from Wincanton. He studied humanities in the College of English Jesuits at St Omer, progressed to the English College in Rome, in 1628, and was ordained priest at the Vatican in 1634. In 1635, having joined the Society of Jesus under the assumed name Maurice Newport, he served in Catholic missions to Hampshire, Devonshire, Oxford and London. He was forced to flee from the capital as a result of the Titus Oates's 'Popish Plot', in 1679, to the Belgian colleges of Ghent and Liege. Eventually, he returned to London where he died, having regained his status as a scholar. His published work included three volumes of poems, dedicated to Charles II in 1665, and a 1671-dated manuscript which passed to the Arundell family archives at Wardour Castle.

Wincanton's past and present claim on the national psyche has largely rested on its strategic position halfway along the main route between London and Cornwall. The line of the principal highway, however, has tended to move with time. In antiquity the Hardway was just what its name implies, being the preferred route down from Salisbury Plain, via Redlynch and Sparkford to the Fosse Way at Ilchester. The present line of the A303 cut the corner, across country, as part of the post-medieval turnpike network. Of more significance, historically, was the course followed by the present A30 which became the Great West Post Road from London to Plymouth. This dropped into Dorset, down Tout Hill at Shaftesbury, and came closest to Wincanton at a salient of Somerset, via a crossroads at Virginia Ash, Henstridge, before re-entering Dorset at Sherborne and continuing through the South Somerset towns of Yeovil, Crewkerne and Chard.

Colonel Roger Whitley, Deputy Postmaster General from 1672 to 1677, was in charge of the Royal Mail service. Whilst on the road, these horse-borne items of post were carried in a leather pouch – 'the post-bag' – with each 'post town' en route having its own bag. Postmasters in the next major town to the east, such as Shaftesbury in the case of Wincanton, had the right to charge for the onward transit of 'by-letters' to neighbouring villages and towns.

Colonel Whitley confirmed in 1673 that the postmaster at Shaftesbury – named as on milestones by its medieval monastic contraction of Shaston – 'could farm all the by-letters, of your stage, with the Wincanton, Bruton, Wells branch etc.' or vice versa. Letters destined for collection at 'receiving houses' in Milborne Port and Queen Camel went via Sherborne. Such arbitrary divisions of the countryside inevitably led to disputes and jealousies. These were fuelled by the fact that long-distance postage was at the lucrative rate of a shilling an ounce, with the person in control of the final stage having everything to play for, as payment was collected on delivery. By 1675, arguments on the division of the spoils caused the arrangements to be revised and Shaftesbury's postmaster lost his principal 'by-letter' traffic for Wells to his counterpart at Yeovil, who also controlled the onward route to Bridgwater in Somerset.

A list of Wincanton's burgesses, dating from 1678, gives the names of the town's taverns and their landlords:

The Angel (Jasper Stacey)
The Crown (Peter Stone)
The Fountain (Peter Stone)
The George (the late William Swanton, died 1671)
The Lion (Benjamin Lewis)

THE SIXTEENTH & SEVENTEENTH CENTURIES

The Queen (Peter Stone)
The Swan (Mr Tucker)
The White Hart (Peter Stone)

For its part in the Duke of Monmouth's disastrous uprising, Wincanton suffered the humiliation of receiving six of those sentenced to be hanged, drawn and quartered for insurrection. They were Thomas Bowden, Richard Harvey, Hugh Holland, William Holland, John Howell and John Tucker. The mass executions took place after Judge George Jeffreys's Bloody Assize reached the Great Hall of Taunton Castle on 17 September 1685. Another local martyr was Richard Harvey, the son of John Harvey and brother of Thomas Harvey, from Suddon.

In 1686, in a War Office survey of the state of the nation following the Monmouth Rebellion, statistics were compiled from each town of their accommodation and stabling. For Somerset, Wells was at the top, with 492 beds in its inns and stabling for 595 horses, and Wincanton was well down the list with just 80 beds but there was stabling for 254 horses.

The distinction of the main event in Wincanton's history must go to what was just about the last military skirmish on English soil during the very violent seventeenth century. About 15 men of King James II's army and eight of their adversaries were killed in a failed attempt at ambushing the advance party of invading forces accompanying Prince William of Orange. He had married Mary Stuart, the British King's daughter, in 1677.

The Dutch landed at Brixham to seize the Stuart throne, on 5 November 1688, in what became known as the Glorious Revolution. It was virtually bloodless by the standards of the time. Opposition took place, however, in the last week of November 1688, in what was then a field, on rising ground beside what was then the eastern end of the High Street. King James's army was riven with conspirators and fence-sitters and the leadership of King, from Salisbury, was compromised by a violent nosebleed. 'Delay facilitated treason,' as the *Dictionary of National Biography* puts it.

The best contemporary description of the Wincanton skirmish is by Revd John Whittle in his *Exact Diary of the late Expedition of the Prince of Orange*. He writes of a small enclosure at the eastern end of the town, on the north side of the road, where there was a dense hedgerow through which most of the firing took place. In the late-seventeenth century the final buildings in the upper High Street would have been much closer to the Market Place than they are now. The eastward extremity of the main High Street was above the former George tavern, on the east side of the present Carrington Way, with lesser buildings intermittently as far uphill as Flinger's Lane and Ireson Lane.

Victorian and Edwardian historian George Sweetman believed the battle must have taken place a short distance further up the slope, from higher ground on the site of Coylton Terrace where the fields began. Somewhere there is a mass grave into which the dead were 'tumbled' together. This was probably in the softer ground of a garden, on the opposite lower side of the road, between Common Road and the present Dolphin Hotel.

John Whittle gives a graphic account of the event:

Now the Prince of Orange, with Prince George of Denmark, the Duke of Ormond, and very many Lords, Knights and Gentlemen, came from Sherborne Castle unto Wincanton and quartered there. This was the place where the first skirmish passed between the two armies; the manner of which I shall impartially relate to the candid and ingenious reader, as I received an account thereof from the minister (Mr Bulgin) and Mr Webb, a Cornet of Horse belonging to the late King James, who was shot there, between his back-bones and reins, and lay desperately ill when we marched by.

A Lieutenant having his post at this town, with about 24 soldiers belonging to the Regiment of the Major-General Mackay [serving the Prince of Orange], hearing that party of Horse belonging to the late King James were posting thither, he was so magnanimous as to resolve to fight them; and in order thereto, posted his men as securely as he could, in a small enclosure, at the east end of the town, on the left [north] side; there was a good hedge between them and the road, which was to defend them against the Horse, and through which they were to fire upon the enemy; but there was a little gate at one corner, and a weak dead hedge.

In this field he [Mackay's Lieutenant] posted most of his men; and on the other side [of] the way, just opposite this place, he posted about six soldiers in a little garden, who had a thick old hedge to cover the from the Horse, and through which they were to fire. The officer [Lieutenant] himself, with four or five men, keeping the road [above the old George tavern].

The enemy's Horse being now advanced within musket-shot, the soldiers would have fired upon them, but the Lieutenant, whose name was Campbell, not knowing what they might be, whether friends or foes, would not permit them, and the more, because a Regiment of Horse belonging to my Lord Cornbury, was come in and joined our forces, and so advancing each towards the other; our officer first gave them the word, saying, 'Stand, stand, for who are ye?'

To which they enemy's officer, at the head of the party of Horse, answered, I am for king James. 'Who are thou for?'

To which our officer replied, 'I am for the Prince of Orange.' 'God damn me,' says the enemy's officer, 'I will Prince thee!'

Whereupon our officer said 'Fire'; and went boldly up to this Popish officer, and shot him in at his mouth and through his brains, so he dropped down dead; our soldiers firing upon them through the hedges on each side, mauled them desperately, and killed several of them.

They carried off their dead presently, being ten to one (for the enemy's party was about 150, and our party but 25). They rode to find out a place to break in upon our men; so some Horse broke in at the upper end of the Croft, some at the lower corner, and others got in at the little gate, which, as is said, was opened by a townsman that stood near the place, so that our men charged as fast as they could to fire upon them, but were now surrounded with the enemy; our soldiers were diverse of them killed.

They defended themselves as well as 'twas possible, for such a handful against so many; and one or two of them being shot in five or so places, were offered quarter by the enemy for their great courage, but they would not accept it from the hands of Papists, and therefore chose rather to die. Now the little company in the garden fired diverse [ways] three times, and the officer, with his men, kept their ground awhile, and then got into the garden to [join] their own party.

The townspeople were much alarmed by this action, and came thronging into the streets; and kind Providence having so ordained it, for the saving our men (else, no doubt, they would all have been cut off, being so mightily overpowered) that a certain Miller came, riding in at the other end of the town [from the west], and hearing of this skirmish, presently reported, that he had overtaken a strong party of Horse belonging to the Prince of Orange, and that he believed they were now entering the town. This was brought to the enemy's ears very quickly, and moreover he called to them, and said, 'Away, for your lives, save yourselves, the enemies are at hand.'

Now these soldiers of the late King James, seeing the people of the town so thick in the streets, running here and there, judged that it might be so, and thereupon they retreated with all speed, galloping away in a confused manner. However, they left more behind killed on their side, than they had killed of our men, for 'twas the judgment of all here that this handful of soldiers (appertaining to his Highness the Prince of Orange) killed more of their enemies than they themselves were in number. There were about 15 tumbled in one grave together, and about eight of our men, the rest being of the enemy's party. Our officers did most of them visit this Mr Webb, Cornet of Horse, to hear the manner of this small action.

The failure of the King's men to hold the line at Wincanton was followed by the arrival of the nation's new leader. On Saturday 1 December 1688 the Prince of Orange was staying at the Dogs in South Street, en route to Westminster and his coronation, as King William III. Sir William Portman of Bryanston, the Jacobite who captured the fugitive Duke of Monmouth in 1685, had changed his loyalties and now provided William's personal escort and guard. Meanwhile, the lines of the main invasion force were closing on Salisbury, from which James II made a hasty exit in the direction of London.

The Dogs, newly built a few years earlier, took its name from a pair of greyhounds carved in stone – the emblem of the Churchey family – mounted on pillars either side of the entrance. The room there where the Prince slept has since been known as the Orange Room. It faces east from above the fine oak staircase, on the first floor, in the south wing of the Dogs. The Prince's host was Richard Churchey who had, until this moment, concealed any involvement in the Duke of Monmouth's ill-fated rebellion that ended with the Battle of Sedgemoor. The treason that dared not speak its name could now be worn as a badge of honour.

The end of his reign – giving rise to the Jacobite toast to 'The little gentleman in black velvet' – came in 1702 when he was no longer of much use and then none at all after his horse stumbled over a molehill.

Time was marked in Wincanton at Dial House, in the Batch, which carries the date 1691 on its sundial, now set on a projecting porch above the pavement. The Bell was one of the town's taverns at this time.

Across the Atlantic, William Dyer junr, the son of Mary and William Dyer, died in Sussex County, Pennsylvania, in 1690. Despite the attrition rate from natural causes and persecution the Dyer name from Wincanton had been successfully planted in the Americas. Among those claiming descent from these 'founders' were the jurist Eliphalet Dyer (1721–1807) who pioneered the settlement of Wyoming Valley; Captain Nehemiah Mayo Dyer (1839–1910) who commanded the *USS Baltimore* in the Battle of Manila Bay; and the dermatologist Isadore Dyer (1865–1920) who established the National Leprosarium.

Cast-iron plate for 'Wincanton 1, Castle Cary 5' on the milestone at Abergavenny.

Chapter Three

The Eighteenth Century

The present buildings on the site of the former Dyer family home at Roundhill Grange, between Wincanton and Bruton, were built in 1701 by James Laurence Churchey as a neat square mansion in classical brick. They replaced those of the grange of the former Stavordale Priory. On Churchey's death, in 1716, it passed to a nephew, Nathaniel Webb, whose family held it until 1830 when another Nathaniel Webb sold the manor-house to George Wyndham.

Buildings at Suddon also date from this time, with it being named Suddon Court by Thomas Gapper (1665–1710), and in due course becoming Suddon Grange.

Storms and fires shaped the redevelopment of Wincanton. The 'Great Storm' of 26–27 November 1703 caused considerable structural damage to substandard thatched and timber buildings. The town's suffering has to be seen in the context of much more tragic news which arrived from elsewhere in the West Country. Off Plymouth, the Eddystone Lighthouse had been swept away, along with its 59-year-old designer Henry Winstanley and his workers, who were there to carry out repairs. That night the Bishop of Bath and Wells and his lady were killed in their bed, by falling masonry, in the Bishop's Palace at Wells. 'Multitudes of cattle' were killed, as well as huge numbers of sheep, including 15,000 across just one section of the Somerset Levels.

The imprint of the 'Great Storm' could still be seen across Wincanton a couple of years later, when 'pockets of dereliction' compounded the effect of 'a devastating blaze' in 1705, and also contributed to the speed in which 'the calamitous fire' on 13 May 1707 leapt from one home to the next. It caused the loss of 44 buildings and was remembered as the 'Great Fire'.

Its spread was also blamed on freeze-dried conditions, from 12 March that year, which were then followed by baking daylight heat. Not only were the wells blocked by debris but subsequent rains swept refuse down Mill Street and put the Town Mills out of business until the autumn. Losses were assessed at £2,900. Philip Bennett (1638–1725) acted as treasurer of a relief fund which raised £636. Bennett had married a Churchey heiress and owned 170 acres in Wincanton as well as land at Cucklington and Motcombe. His name lives on at Southgate, on the town's first modern trading estate, at Bennett's Mead and Bennett's Field.

Pestilence was another recurrent peril with smallpox ravaging the town in a series of epidemics. In that of 1711, a particularly virulent outbreak, the disease claimed 88 lives.

The big fire of South Street took place on 10 April 1722 when Dragoons passing through the town led rescue operations. Their bravery was rewarded with beer at the Bear Inn which had been built two years earlier.

Those of a different persuasion, when it came to alcohol, held the town's first recorded Quaker meeting in 1722. Stukeley's Bank (otherwise known as Stuckey's Bank) dates from 1724.

Ireson House in Grant's Lane was built in 1726 by architect and delftware potter Nathaniel Ireson (1685–1769). He came to the town from Warwickshire and it was at his instigation that the parish church was partially rebuilt. Inscriptions record that the south aisle was reconstructed in the time of churchwardens George Deane and John Pike, in 1735, by mason John Clewett. In 1748, Ireson worked on the fourteenth-century church tower, installing a clock and five bells, and presented the altar to commemorate re-roofing the building. Nathaniel Ireson died on 18 April 1769 and is buried in the churchyard, beneath a pedestal surmounted by a life-sized statue, cast in artificial stone.

In 1727, from 'the capacious chimney corner' of the George Inn in Castle Cary, a travelling sailor began questioning the landlord about 'the families of note residing at Wincanton'. He visibly shuddered at the mention of 'old Mogg at the Dogs'. Although tired, he said he was determined to proceed to Wincanton, and paid taverner Richard Palmer with a doubloon from a purse heavy with foreign silver. These were his last wages, he explained, which had been augmented by ransacking Spanish ports. They shook hands, as the mariner lifted his portmanteau, and went off alone into the wet night.

The following morning a bludgeoned body, finally dispatched by a knife wound to the heart, was found by the roadside midway between Castle Cary and Wincanton. As was the custom, on being taken away, the corpse was placed in the porch of the nearest town church, which was St Peter and St Paul in Wincanton. On hearing of the crime, Richard Palmer came from Castle Cary, to view the body. He confirmed to grey-haired rector Revd George Plunkett that this was his sailor guest from the previous evening.

Suspicion soon fell upon the ostler (stableman) from the George – namely Jack White – and its buildings were searched. Hay in the stable loft concealed the sailor's portmanteau and his leather bag of doubloons. The sailor's family Bible identified him as William White, the son of John and Mary White of the Dogs, who had been baptised by a much younger

Above: *Wincanton's one and only life-size statue, to delftware potter Nathaniel Ireson who died at the age of 83 in 1769, photographed in 1991.*

Right: *Romanesque terracotta, sculpted by Nathaniel Ireson's own hands, beginning to look its age in 2004.*

Ireson House from the south, overlooking the High Street, from Ireson Lane.

Revd George Plunkett on 2 February 1692. A certificate to this effect, counter-signed by parish clerk Thomas Green, had been pasted on the end-papers. It was endorsed by town worthies Abraham Gapper, Robert Coombs and Emma Ireson, who acted as sponsors.

It was soon established that the deceased William White was the brother of Jack White. These last two known descendants of the early medieval Le Blanc family had fallen out over their lost inheritance. Jack White confessed to the internecine crime and the law took its course. He was hanged at Taunton Castle.

Because of 'the wicked nature of the unnatural offence' his body was returned to the scene of the crime for final humiliation as a public warning. It was suspended in chains from a gibbet until the bones were picked clean by birds and maggots and scoured by the elements. Long after the skeleton had fallen apart, the shaft and arm of the gibbet survived, and the stump stood long into the nineteenth century. The spot is known to this day as Jack White's Gibbet. Its actual site is said to be on the south-east corner of the crossroads, towards a suitably spooky strip of woodland, and lies in the parish of Bratton Seymour. The practice of gibbeting was carried out by custom, rather than through the judicial process, and was not legally recognised until 1752. It was abolished in 1834.

Rodber House, beside the Batch between the River Cale and West Hill, was built or rebuilt by Nathaniel Ireson in the early 1730s. Simon Webb, who married lawyer's daughter Martha King, was living there in 1736. Simon Webb was a churchwarden in 1743–44 and Poor Law Overseer in 1750. He died on 6 March 1775 and his widow, Martha Webb, followed on 8 November 1776. Their son William Webb lived in Rodber House until his death there at the age of 69 on 28 April 1819.

Rockhill House, in North Street, also dates from the 1730s. It appears to have been built by Bartholomew Day and was at the cutting edge of architectural fashion in being the earliest Wincanton building to incorporate Bath-stone dressings. The imposing three-storey building, with extensive cellars and attics, also shows a continental connection rare in provincial England. All its windows are precisely a metre wide. Most houses at this time were the product of jobbing builders but Rockhill House had a professional architect.

A total of 140 properties qualified for the Poor Rate levied on 10 December 1736 by churchwardens George Deane and John Pike and overseers John Clewett and Michael Vining. The total raised 'for the relief of the poor in the parish of Wincanton' was £364.1s.5d. The document provides the following list of taverns in the town:

Bear Inn (John Webb)
Bell Inn, South Street (Mr Plucknett)
Black Lion (Bernard James)
Golden Lion (William Day)

Ireson also provided for the future, with 16 panels for subsequent members of the family, but only a few were inscribed before they became extinct.

The Lamb (Robert Pearce)
White Horse (George Deane)

The Dorset and Somerset Canal was set to come through the town but was never built. It was intended to lead from the Somerset coalfield, via Wincanton, in the first stage of an ambitious plan to cut off the South-West peninsula – and its hazardous coastline around Land's End – by linking the Avon Gorge with Poole Harbour. Revd Samuel Farewell summoned a meeting of enthusiastic Somerset landowners and chaired the discussion in Wincanton, in March 1739:

It was resolved that a communication by an inland navigation between Bristol and Poole will be of the greatest advantage both to the landed and commercial interests of this county and that proper measures be taken for carrying the same into execution.

Two different lines have been proposed for conducting the inland navigation. One, from Bath to Frome, and thence to Wincanton and Henstridge, Stalbridge, Bagber (with a communication to Sturminster Newton), Kings Stag bridge, Plush, Piddletrenthide and Puddletown to Wareham, from whence there is a

The symbolic skull at Nathaniel Ireson's feet.

communication with Poole Harbour. The other also from Bath, in the same line, as far as Stalbridge, from thence by Sturminster Newton, Blandford, and Wimborne, to Canford, and from hence to the town of Poole, or as near to the several places above mentioned as the nature of the ground will admit.

It is received that before any positive determination respecting the line of the canal be fixed on, some eminent surveyor or surveyors, engineers, or other proper persons be appointed to take the necessary levels, and make proper calculations and estimates of the expenses likely to incurred, as well as of the tonnage likely to arise on the lines respectively proposed and to report to a committee to be appointed.

The earliest mention of Nathaniel Ireson's pottery works at Wincanton comes from 1739. Evidence of his building activities can be found in the Parish Register, on 13 August 1741, which records the accidental death of John Hacker who was killed at Ireson's quarry on Windmill Hill by a stone which fell from a wagon.

Other unfortunates, at a time when poverty was at average rather than acute levels, are recorded in the roll of Wincanton Workhouse. There were 64 inmates from the parish in residence on 22 April 1742. George Sweetman noted a century and a half later that their ages were well below the norm for Victorian times and also that a significant proportion had Puritan Christian names. Many were the descendants of Roundheads rather than Royalists:

John Bratcher (7), Judith Bratcher (37), Kate Bratcher (4), Samuel Bratcher (38), Samuel Bratcher (2), Ann Brine (40), Robert Brine (7), Benjamin Clement (3), Sarah Day (6), John Edgell (40), Edward Goddard (7), John Goddard (9), Mary Goddard (8), Jane Hine (56), John Humphreys (12), Samuel Humphreys (10), Elizabeth Hurman (8), Abraham Ivie (4), John Ivie (infant), Patience Ivie (37), Sarah Ivie (7), Anne Lumber (6), Judith Lumber (7), Mary Lumber (9), Katherine Lumber (33), Richard Lumber (6), John Manning (9), Mary Mogg (60), Abraham Munday (10), Hannah Munday (4), John Munday (7), Jane Newman (54), John Newman (15), Stephen Newman (12), Elizabeth Oatley (8), Mary Parker (40), Elizabeth Pauley (80), Ann Parsons (6), Elizabeth Parsons (7), Elizabeth Pauley (80), Repentance Parsons (62), Henry Read (75), George Stone (16), Sarah Stone (57), William Stone (45), Edith Thick (10), Mary Thick (7), Elisha Vining (3), Love Vining (10), Samuel Vining (5), William Vining (9), Ann Watts (28), Ann Watts (infant), Benjamin White (5), Daniel White (9), Elizabeth White (7), Mary White (7), Tabitha White (33), William White (2), Ann Willis (13), Sarah Willis (2), William Willis (8), Christopher Wimbolt (42), and Timothy Wimbolt (9).

George Neville, Earl of Abergavenny, is said to have married a member of the Zouch family and thereby acquired an interest in the manor of Wincanton. This connection led to the naming of roadside cottages and the gate across the highway just beyond the milestone a mile west of the town, between West Hill and Holbrook. Occupied by John Pike and family, in 1745, the cottages became known as Abergavenny.

The town's next big blaze, in 1747, gave added momentum to rebuilding projects in the town. Lofty buildings of brick and stone, with tiled roofs, were now in vogue. The town's distinctive high windows served a practical purpose in maximising the light for weaving Dowlas cloth. Its raw material, flax, was grown locally, as was *Cannabis sativa* (hemp) for rope and sail-cloth. By the close of the eighteenth century there were more than 200 looms and spinning wheels in operation across Wincanton and Bayford.

Wincanton attorney Richard Ring represented a consortium of 62 townspeople (including himself) who pooled resources to prosecute those perpetrating 'several larcenies and felonius acts' including the mutilation of cows 'by cutting their manes and tails' and the 'clandestine' sabotage of 'several fruit trees and other trees likely to become timber, and garden fruits'.

The level of damage seems to have been of anti-social proportions rather than anything more serious. It seems it have been an indication of urban unrest rather than rural revolution. Signatories were:

John Andrews, Richard Andrews, John Brickenden, Nicholas Brown, Joseph Clewett, Robert Combe, Thomas Coombes, Charles Creed, John Cross, George Deane, Jonathan Dove, Peter Dove, Richard Edwards, Robert Gapper, Thomas Goodfellow, John Guyer, Thomas Harris, John Horler, Samuel Horler, John Hurd, John Hurman, William Hussey, Nathaniel Ireson, Andrew Ivie, Charles Ivie, William Jewell, John King, Mary Kite, Charles Lewis, Richard Lewis, John Mansfield, Edward Matthews, John Mitchell, William Mogg, John Norman, William Oatley, John Parsons, Joseph Parsons, Robert

Pearce, Robert Perfect, Thomas Perry, John Pike, John Pitman, Philip Pitman, Stephen Pitman, Henry Plucknett, John Richardson, Richard Ring, John Rogers, Richard Simpson, Thomas Slade, Philip Smith, Timothy Taylor, Joseph Vining, Joshua Vining, Robert Wadman, Moses Walter, William Way, Jonathan Webb, Simon Webb, Thomas White, and William Winter.

The chancel of the parish church was rebuilt by Nathaniel Ireson in 1748. He also designed and paid for the adding of the clerestory. Writing in 1792, clergyman and historian John Collinson records that Revd George Farewell was the 'present incumbent' at Wincanton. This was an error, however, as it was Revd Samuel Farewell from Holbrook who bought Rousewell House near the parish church for his Parsonage. The remainder of Collinson's account is accurate:

The church is dedicated to St. Peter and St. Paul, and is a pretty large edifice, plain without, but very handsome within; the chancel having been rebuilt, and the church new roofed and windowed in 1748. It is 92 feet in length, and 52 feet in breadth, consisting of a nave, chancel, north and south aisles, all except the chancel covered with lead. At the west end is a plain square tower, containing a clock and five bells.

By about 1750 the direct line of the Farewell family at Holbrook House had died out, and the estate was in the ownership of a member of the Hallett family, but he assumed the Farewell name to perpetuate the connection. It was from this later line of Farewells that Holbrook's most famous son was born.

Francis George Farewell was born at Holbrook in 1784. His father, Revd Samuel Farewell who was rector of Wincanton, died in 1797. This caused the family to move to Tiverton where Francis became a day scholar at Blundell's School. He left at the age of 13 to become a midshipman in the Royal Navy. That was in 1807 and Farewell re-enters our story in 1824.

The landscaping of the parkland grounds at Holbrook House dates from the Farewell centuries, including its giant cedar of Lebanon, a species which is not recorded in John Evelyn's *Silva* of 1664 and makes its earliest documentary appearance in Britain with a planting at Bretby Park, Derbyshire, in 1676. Seedlings were planted in many English parks towards the end of the seventeenth century – including that at Holbrook – and they have grown into the most stately trees in Europe.

Young solicitor Moulton Messiter (1704–86) moved to Wincanton from Maiden Bradley after marrying lawyer's daughter Mary Ring in June 1754. They had 14 children, of whom Richard Messiter was the eldest son. The family acquired several High Street properties, and then Coneygore, in 1773.

John Wesley (1703–91) took advantage of the Toleration Act but preached against the extension of religious freedom to Roman Catholics. The founder of Methodism first visited Wincanton in 1762. Being 'practically the only itinerating clergyman' he found himself in ever-increasing demand from newly formed societies across the country. By 1784, there were a total of 359 Wesleyan chapels, served by 100 travelling preachers, but all wanted to hear Wesley. His presence was immediate, charismatic, with a slim frame and eyes 'the brightest and most piercing that can be conceived'.

The old Market House on the south side of the Shambles – the building with the butchers' benches – in the centre of the town was in 'a ruinous condition' when it was demolished in 1767. The feoffees (parish trustees) were enraged that this had been done without their authorisation. They resolved 'to punish with the utmost vigour, the person or persons concerned' but accepted the reality of the situation and proceeded to acquire and remove adjacent dilapidated cottages which were owned by church charities.

The site beside the Shambles became a new Market House with a Town Hall above, completed in 1769 at a cost of £400, and incorporating a tiny 'blind-house or lock-up' which was known as the Roundhouse. The latter remained in use until the building of a Police Station in 1860.

In 1768 a group of townspeople signed a pact to bear mutual financial responsibility in bringing to justice those responsible for 'diverse robberies, burglaries, felonies and other misdemeanours and offences' that had been 'lately done and committed'. As with a similar exercise in 1749, the list of signatories gives us a record of the wealthiest residents, although only 40 signed this time:

Richard Andrews, William Bracher junior, Thomas Brickenden, John Brown, Nicholas Brown, Margaret Burges, William Chaffey, Joseph Clewett, Robert Combe, John Deane, Elizabeth Dove, Isiah Farrington, Robert Gapper, Edward Goddard, Thomas Goodfellow, John Guyer, James Kiddle, John Harris, William Harvey, John Hurd, Thomas Hussey, Andrew Ivie, John Leach, Jane Lewis, Richard Lewis, Moulton Messiter, John Mitchell senior, John Mitchell junior, John Parsons, Joseph Parsons, Edward Pearce, Robert Perfect, Jonathan Pitman, Philip Pittman, Stephen Pittman, Thomas Slade, Robert Wadman, William Way, Nathaniel Webb, and William Winter.

The Window Tax, in operation from 1695 until its repeal and replacement in 1851, was implemented on

IRESON LANE
LEADING TO
GRANTS LANE

COMMON ROAD

Right: *Castle Cottage in Common Road, with bizarre Gallic flourishes, credited to French prisoners in the early-nineteenth century.*

Left: *Wincanton Toll House, looking eastwards up Bayford Hill, before the removal in 1874 of the high iron gates across both the top end of the High Street* (centre) *and the junction with Common Road* (right).

The reception for the Prince of Wales, later King Edward VIII, who passed through Wincanton on 19 July 1923.

THE EIGHTEENTH CENTURY

Present-day lines of the Toll House – its angular projection into the street was removed after the abolition of pay roads in 1874 – on the corner of Common Road and the High Street.

Southgate Road, looking westwards up Tout Hill in 1897, with the children standing in front of the former South Gate turnpike cottages.

Bennett's Field Trading Estate (centre) *and the site of the new Fire Station* (left) *from the former railway embankment in 1985.*

The crossroads at the Tything (centre) *in 1991, from the wall of the former Milk Factory, showing the old Fire Station on the corner of Southgate Road and Moor Lane* (centre right).

THE EIGHTEENTH CENTURY

an escalating scale. In this sense it was fair, but like any tax it was unpopular, and could be circumvented by blocking windows or designing sham windows for new properties. In 1774, Thomas Hellier (three windows) and widow Hannah Andrews (six windows) were charged the 9d. minimum. Mrs Bennett (10) had to pay 2s.10d., William Bracher (20) 8s.8d., and James Beacon (24) 12s.3d. The principal houses in the town, in descending order of size, were occupied by:

James Beacon at the Bear Inn (24) 12s.3d.
William Bracher (20) 8s.4d.
Martha Ireson at Ireson House (19) 7s.10d.
Moulton Messiter (19) 7s10d.
Richard Ring (19) 7s10d.
John Thorne, junior (19) 7s.10d.
John Deane at the White Horse (18) 7s.6d.
Thomas Slade (18) 7s.6d.
Mr Way (18) 7s.6d.
Robert Carrier at the White Hart (17) 7s.1d.
Thomas Ellis (17) 7s.1d.
Israel Lush (16) 6s.9d.
Isiah Farrington (15) 6s.4d.
Miss Lewis, dressmaker (15) 6s.4d.
John Guyer (14) 6s.0d.
William Harvey (14) 6s.0d.
Mary Kiddle (14) 6s.0d.
Robert Perfect (14) 6s.0d.
Charles Lovell (13) 5s.1d.
William Day at the Black Lion (part, 13) 5s.1d.
Thomas Brooks (12) 4s.3d.
David Little (12) 4s.3d.
Mrs Dove (11)
Edward Pearce (11) 3s.6d.
Mr Tewkesbury (11) 3s.6d.
Mrs Bennett (10) 2s.10d.
Mrs Day (10)
Edmund Hussey (10) 2s.10d.
John Keates (10) 2s.10d.
Mr Mitchell (10) 2s.10d.
John White (10) 2s.10d.
(and 83 smaller properties)

In the intensely cold winter of 1788, when the River Thames froze over, charity began at home. That December a public appeal raised £33.0s.6d. to help feed the poor. A total of 190 adults and 284 children (from 73 families) – representing a quarter of the town – benefited from the fund-raising. Bacon and pease pudding was distributed, along with 910 loaves of bread, and 1,205 pounds of beef.

South Bank House on Bayford Hill, at 395 feet above the Blackmore Vale, went on the market as 'a genteel new-built dwelling house' in 1789. It was bought by Revd John Messiter. Half a century later it

Attentive response to a canine photo-call for the Blackmore Vale Hunt, meeting outside the Value Spot Domestic Bazaar in about 1930.

The Tanker Depot (centre) and western end of Southgate Road, south-eastwards from West Hill to the snowy ridge between Cucklington and Buckhorn Weston on 1 February 1985 (the temperature was -2 degrees Centigrade).

Left: *Wiring up the new lamp standard, on the site of the former well head, in August 1991.*

Below: *West side of the Market Place in 1902, featuring the shop fronts of shoemaker Edwin Harris* (left), *Hutchings & Son country tailors* (centre), *and Belben's* (right) *on the North Street corner.*

was the home of George Messiter who enlarged it upwards and northwards in 1848.

By 1790, one portion of the manor of Wincanton had passed via Mary Yeatman of Hinton St Mary to Revd Harry Farr Yeatman of Stock Gaylard, the deer park at Lydlinch, and Uriah and George Messiter. Another moiety of the manor was held by the Seymour family, from Edward Seymour in 1789, to his descendant Harry Seymour a century later. At the Dogs the Churcheys were followed by the Mogg, Biggin and Deanesly families.

Toll highways were now in vogue, replacing and upgrading routes that were still basically a combination of prehistoric ridgeways with Roman roads, altered at the edges a millennium later to provide access to the great monastic houses. The local Turnpike Trust gates were at Willoughby Hedge between Mere and Hindon; East Gate between Bayford Hill and the High Street in Wincanton; South Gate near Hawker's Bridge, or Aucres Bridge, which dated from before 1652; and Abergavenny Gate at Suddon Farm, on the Castle Cary road. After deducting the expenses of labour, maintenance and collection costs, they returned the following profits in 1791:

Willoughby Hedge Gate – £200.2s.1d.
South Gate, Wincanton – £146.9s.2d.
East Gate, Wincanton – £131.3s.10d.
Abergavenny Gate – £45.19s.2d.

Eight houses were destroyed by a fire in the High Street in 1794. Tout Hill House was built in about 1795 on the site of the Mansion House. This had been bought by Thomas Gapper, from Samuel Barrett in 1752, and remained in the family until the death of Thomas Aubrey Gapper, in 1886. George Green became Wincanton's first recorded centenarian in 1795, and died on 3 January 1798, at the age of 102.

Distress and discontent followed in the wake of the Wincanton Enclosure Acts which deprived the poor and the public of hundreds of acres of common land on either side of what became a totally enclosed Common Road. Only the feoffees, acting as trustees of the town's fairs and markets, were conceded a token area at Batchpool which was conveyed to them as an allotment. Stavordale Fair was still being held in its historic venue, on Wincanton Common, on 5 August 1793.

Wincanton's countryside is still largely pastoral, with the town being home to the major tanker depot for gathering the region's milk, but the land hereabouts was formerly of importance for more than its cows. Published in 1797, John Billingsley's *General View of the Agriculture of the County of Somerset*, could advise on the cultivation of female cannabis plants without any mention of statutory difficulties. The Somerset and Dorset cordage industry was making the sails and ropes that would bring the nation its victory off Cape Trafalgar in 1805:

In the rich fertile country, extending from Wincanton through Yeovil, to Crewkerne, flax and hemp are cultivated in great abundance, the value of which is in proportion to the skill and spirit with which it is cultivated.

Fields around Wincanton were also notable for the large-scale production of turnips. All three cash crops became extinct during the nineteenth century and many of the fields reverted to grass, although some were ploughed again under wartime Cultivation Orders in 1940–45 when import restrictions caused a revival of flax growing and sky-blue fields were among the colours of southern England at war. Vice-Admiral William Fookes, Rear Admiral of the Blue in Nelson's Royal Navy, died at Holbrook House in 1798.

The Congregational Chapel in Mill Street, reached by an alleyway between and behind terraced cottages and their gardens, was built by Revd William Warlow in 1799 at a cost of £837. Despite its cramped position, it claimed to accommodate 400, and there was sufficient ground for a graveyard. The building was merely a chapel, Congregationalists insisted, 'and those who gather inside it comprise the church.' The distinction became instantly blurred and still causes confusion.

Eastwards in the rain from the rooftop of No. 5 Market Place, up the High Street towards Windmill Hill in 1929, three decades before demolition of the Rectory (left centre).

Uphill from the Market Place in 1905, into the High Street between 'K' Shoes (left) and Latcham's Printing Works (right).

Left: *Newly erected Bath-stone plinth and lamp standard, looking into North Street, in August 1991.*

Below: *The south side of the Market Place, from the Red Lion (left) to Kenneth Lawson's Saddlery (centre) and the top end of Church Street in 1985.*

✧ THE EIGHTEENTH CENTURY ✧

Eastwards from the Market Place into the High Street from the Midland Bank (far left) *to Lloyds Bank* (far right) *in 1985.*

A cyclist turns right off the old A303 in the centre of town in 1950, into the Market Place, where the shop fronts include Sally Lunn's Café, Edwin Harris' shoes and the Value Spot.

Parish pump and the Shambles (centre left) *projecting into what is now the highway, after completion of the Town Hall tower* (background) *in 1878, with the Red Lion Inn adjoining* (right).

The awning of Broughton's newsagents and fish and chip shop, down to the Red Lion in the 1990s.

Wincanton in bloom, across to window boxes at the Red Lion and the office of Somerton & Frome Conservative Association above.

The Post Office and Market Place, westwards into Mill Street, in 2000.

THE EIGHTEENTH CENTURY

High Street butcher Reginald Shave (left) *striding past Williams newsagents and tobacconists opposite the International Stores* (centre) *and Town Hall* (right) *in the 1950s.*

Right: *Moss Pharmacy, still carrying its earlier name of Knight & Son, framed by the Greyhound arch.*

A Rolls Royce climbing from Church Street into the Market Place in 2004.

Above: *The frontage of the Greyhound when this former coaching inn was on the market in the 1990s.*

Right: *Royal arms (centre), commemorating the stay of Princess Victoria, above the entrance to Greyhound Yard.*

Below: *Cobbled way beside Greyhound Mews, south to the Town Hall clock tower (centre top), above the arch into the Market Place.*

Below right: *Victorian ladies step off the coach in Wincanton, beside the Bear Inn, at the end of the longest reign on record in 1901.*

Chapter Four
The Nineteenth Century

There were at least 200 loom workers in Wincanton in 1800. Flax was bleached white, by boiling in furnaces, and spun into thread for linen. Rows of weaving sheds linked the bottom ends of Church Street and Mill Street and also ran parallel to Silver Street. They continued around the corner, on the south side, as the highway turned beside the entrance to the Town Mills towards the River Cale and the Batch.

The first national census revealed that there were 381 families in the town in 1801, with an average size of five adults, totalling 1,772 inhabitants. Of these, 1,064 were employed in trade, 586 in agriculture, and the remaining 140 incapacitated, retired or otherwise unemployed.

Richard Messiter (1759–1830), who followed in his father's steps as a solicitor, raised a troop of Volunteer Infantry and was then captain of a troop of the East Somerset Yeomanry until the respite of the Peace of Amiens in 1802. He married Mary Brickell from Shaftesbury and became involved in politics there, until bankruptcy forced him to cross the Atlantic, where he died at Newburg, New York.

Wincanton's short fame as a spa town began in 1805 with the commercial exploitation of two mineral springs on what was a detached manor of the parish

Knight & Son (left) *and the Town Hall clock tower, across from the Bear Hotel, proclaiming the Edwardian new age of garages and the Automobile Association.*

of Horsington, around the hamlet of Horwood. Physicwell House, with pump-room, plunge baths, and lodging-house, claimed a water quality equivalent to that at Cheltenham. In social ambience, however, Wincanton failed to compete in the higher fashion stakes. The speculative venture collapsed, its cachet and kudos having been squandered, and the architectural rescue of its half-hidden facilities had to await gentrification in the 1980s.

There was also a Horwood Well Bank, with a banking house in a field towards Snag Farm, which issued notes for a short period, from 1807 to 1810. Edmund Griffith, Donovan & Company, who also traded from the town as the Wincanton Bank, then declared themselves insolvent. This coincided with the reported robbery of £1,881 in bank notes, from a Wincanton safe, which cynics regarded as fraud.

The Dogs was among the buildings that housed French prisoners in the Napoleonic Wars. Until the overriding fashion for wallpaper, several High Street houses had their murals of vineyards and other pastoral French scenes, produced by an officer-dominated group that brought suave tastes to the town. Many arrived after Nelson's famous naval victory off Cape Trafalgar in October 1805. Wincanton and Crediton, Devon, were chosen as suitable medium-sized towns for holding prisoners of war, out of sight of the coast. Wall building became their occupational therapy.

Three militia companies of Somerset Infantry Volunteers formed in Wincanton, after a muster in August 1803, when the 1st Corps was established. Its officers were Captain Uriah Messiter and Lieutenant Richard Ring, as adjutant, and they commanded 49 men. The 2nd Corps was led by Captain Robert Gapper and enrolled 67 men. The 3rd Corps followed, under Captain William Webb, with 60 men.

Two ages come together in this turn of the twentieth century photograph. The initial letters of 'Pit & Garage' can be glimpsed in the background. The Bear was a pit-stop for the first motor cars to attempt the long haul from London to the West.

The old Town Hall (centre left, destroyed by fire on 10 August 1877) and the Shambles (centre right, demolished 1878), projecting into what is now the main road, in a view from the east, c.1870.

Old Wincantonians William Rumbold (left foreground) and Roy Sansom fronting a living history forum at the Town Hall in 2005.

Above: *Town Hall lighting conductor and 1878-dated weathervane, pointing south, plus a flock of starlings in 2004.*

Below left: *The Town Hall clock tower from the north-west, from the York stone-sets and lamp standard above a floral horse trough given to the town by 'A Friend of Animals', Miss Annie Scammell, in 1930.*

Below: *Built in 1878 and 'Restored 1977', the north (left) and east-facing (right) sides of the Town Hall clock tower in 2001.*

✣ THE NINETEENTH CENTURY ✣

Westwards down the High Street to the sign of saddler Henry James at No. 17 and the Rectory (centre), from the Post Office at No. 20 (far left) and the Hospital at No. 18 (centre left), outside which are Edwardian ladies and boys in 1903.

Eastwards up the High Street from the home of solicitor John Oliver Cash (left) and the Rectory, opposite Charles Henry Woodcock's garage (centre right), advertising Shell lubricating oils and petrol in 1906.

There was a natural event, locally, to take minds momentarily off the national situation. Huge hailstones pounded Wincanton in 1808. The record specimen was three inches in diameter and 9.75 inches in circumference.

The census of 1811 shows there were 2,156 people living in Wincanton, of whom 306 were prisoners of war. Others have their graves in St Peter and St Paul's churchyard. Far from being held under house arrest, the Frenchmen were restrained 'by their honour', on a pledge not to escape. Some may have tried. George Culliford was committed to Ilchester Gaol, from Wincanton, in August 1811 on a charge of having attempted to smuggle French captives out of the country.

For air and exercise the Frenchmen were allowed to walk out of town in daylight hours for a mile in each direction. These points were marked by Abergavenny Gate on the Castle Cary road, Anchor Bridge on the main road to the south-west, Bayford Elm to the east, and Gooselands Farm northwards at Charlton Musgrove.

One wonders if such restrictions were stretched to enable the crossing of Anchor Bridge and continuing 100 yards to the Anchor Inn, facing the junction with the road to Lattiford and Templecombe, from the north side of the main road. The sign of the Anchor must have seemed particularly inviting – as it signified the turning for the coast – and the building is now under the tarmac of the A357 which heads for the ports of Poole and Cherbourg. Anchor Inn, at a road junction rather than a hamlet, was a travellers' tavern, well known to sailors and smugglers.

The Frenchmen's recreation room in Wincanton was a building in Oborn's Yard. The first marriage between one of the officers and a local girl was that between John Peter Pichou and Dinah Edwards, from Bayford, at Stoke Trister parish church in 1808. By 1810 the United Fraternity of Free and Accepted Masons of England had given its approval to the Grand Lodge of France authorising the establishment of a French Masonic Lodge in Wincanton. Among those who stayed in the town, setting up businesses, was Alberto Bioletti who had a hairdressers and watch shop in South Street, in 1830.

The surgeon son of Richard Ring from Wincanton, John Ring (1752–1821) met Dr Edward Jenner in August 1799, and proceeded to devote his professional life to the cause of vaccination. In 1808 he joined a 'pistol-packing party' that went to Ringwood to confront potentially violent protesters and convince them that there was no danger from using cowpox inoculations to prompt antibodies which protected against the much more dangerous smallpox virus.

The British Vaccine Establishment was founded in 1809, under Jenner's directorship, and employed Ring as its principal vaccinator and inspector of vaccination stations. John Ring was then ousted by James Moore, in an act of preferment instigated by his brother General Sir John Moore, and Edward Jenner resigned in protest. 'Honest John Ring' was credited by Jenner with having vaccinated tens of thousands of persons. Ring published a number of medical tracts including *A Treatise on the Gout* in 1811 and *A Caution against Vaccine Swindlers and Impostors* in 1816.

In 1815, 42-year-old Wincanton blacksmith Samuel Daw was convicted of stealing woollen and linen drapery and sentenced to transportation for seven years. He was marched from Dorchester Castle Gaol to the *Laurel* hulk in Portsmouth Harbour on 20 May 1817 to await shipment to New South Wales. He left behind a wife and five children.

His favourite watering hole had been the Hit and Miss at the bottom end of Mill Street which was known as the 'Black Hole of Calcutta'. This was a reference to the notorious Black Hole Prison – a dungeon only 18 feet square – into which 146 Britons

41

Above: Donkey cart and wheelbarrow as street traffic in about 1904, looking eastwards from what are now the portals of the HSBC (left) and the sign of saddler Henry James, opposite London House, to the shop front of tobacconist and confectioner Robert Bassett at No. 16 (centre).

Left: Railway delivery dray coming up from the station in 1905, passing the White Horse Hotel and Bear Hotel, with the group of children outside the home of solicitor John Oliver Cash.

Charles Woodcock & Son's garage at No. 8 High Street with a 1925-dated 'Michelin man' above the arch and 'Sold' signs on the two Morrises (Flatnose and Bullnose), looking up the street to another Flatnose parked outside Ash House.

THE NINETEENTH CENTURY

Westwards down the street from No. 18 (left) and Salisbury's Antiques at No. 17 (right) with the shop fronts of Eldridge Pope, Surridge Dawson, Weatherheads, Sydney Brock & Son and Clementina, in 1984.

were crammed on 20 June 1756 by Indian insurgents. Only 23 came out alive the following morning. The name was transferred to the nearby George Inn after this was opened by William Lindsey in 1836. Mrs Court, widow of Sid Court who was a former tenant of the George, recorded in 1984 that its local name in the mid-twentieth century was 'The Fleapit'.

The toll-road south from Bruton to Wincanton, and onwards to Sherborne, was constructed by Bruton Turnpike Trust in 1818. Its progress caused or coincided with the enclosure of Barrow Common, at Charlton Musgrove, in sight of Roundhill Grange. At the same time the Wincanton Turnpike Trust modernised the track eastwards through a string of commons towards and beyond Hunter's Lodge.

Among those who found Wincanton by their wayside was John Parker, 1st Earl of Morley (1772–1840), en route from the House of Lords to his Saltram Castle seat. It was the evening of 15 November 1820. Henry Richard Vassall Fox, 3rd Baron Holland (1773–1840), wrote a ditty about 'Time's anarchy without a clock' based on the town's public timepiece being out of action. Their lordships' stay for the night had been disrupted by the confusion caused by its absence:

The cook has scarcely dipped the chine,
When all the neighbours met to dine.
The town behaves as never town did;
'tis all confusion, worse confounded.
No bargain's kept, no hour is certain,
At midnight one undraws the curtain.
I saw another wake at one,
And ask about the rising Sun.
What does it mean? The clock is dumb.

Benjamin Day from Wincanton was hanged for burglary, at Ilchester Gaol, on 1 May 1822. His body was returned to the town for burial but no funeral service was held.

Wincanton-born Francis George Farewell, from Holbrook House, was playing a part in the creation of the British Empire. Silas Ellis painted the scene in southern Africa at 'the founding of the first trading station at Port Natal by Lieutenant Francis George Farewell RN, August 1824'.

Zulu power had been established there in about 1812 and there was fighting with British settlers. Haydn's *Victorian Dictionary of Dates* gives 1823 as the year that 'Lieut. Farewell with some emigrants settled'. The Dutch had already attempted to colonise Natal. It was formally annexed as a British possession and became a Crown colony in 1856. Not that Francis Farewell lived to see the Union Jack proclaiming sovereignty over Natal. He split his time between there and Cape Town. At the end of 1829 he was back in Natal and although he had been on friendly terms with the locals, who knew him as Feban Ka Mjoji, there was a bout of unrest and Farewell was killed in a skirmish.

Six-year-old Princess Victoria, with her mother the Duchess of Kent, stayed at the Greyhound Hotel in 1825 while en route between Kensington Palace and their seaside home at Sidmouth.

The young William Barnes (1801–90), a schoolmaster before he won regional acclaim as Dorset's parson poet, established his Chantry House Academy in Mere in 1827. It broke new ground in being doubly unusual as a boarding institution. Firstly, it had an intellectual rather than a sporting ethos, with no physical regime. Secondly, discipline was achieved by reproach rather than the rod. In the quaint old Wiltshire market town, Barnes found an alleyway with a 'Gate a vallen to' and relict apple trees among the limes of 'Linden Lea', in settings that survive to this day.

Where Mere disappointed William and young wife Julia was in having 'a society much inferior to that of Dorchester'. Instead Julia put her energy into starting a family, with daughters being born in 1829 and 1833, and William devoted his evenings to writing dialect poetry and a rather plodding drama.

Mere lacked a suitable venue, so the Wincanton Theatre hosted the premier of 'The Blasting of Revenge, or Justice for the Just' on 27 April 1831. It was billed as an 'entire new drama, written by Mr Barnes, Master of the Academy at Mere.' Barnes attended, to receive only short and subdued applause, and none of his short-lived series of plays managed to make the desired transition and transfer to the London stage.

Wincanton also enters into the story of William Barnes by providing the catalyst for what became the next stage of his academic career. Holbrook House was the home of retired Major-General Henry Shrapnel (1751–1842), whose name went into the dictionary, for having invented the exploding shell. It is clear from their social evenings together that the dialect poet was no pacifist, nor a social revolutionary, as they concurred in the summer of 1834 on the

43

Eastwards up the High Street in 1984 with the Midland Bank (left) facing the frontages of Eldridge Pope wine merchants, Surridge Dawson wholesale newsagents, Weatherhead's drapery in London House, Ash House and Sarum Furnishing & Bedding Co. Ltd.

The blind of John Eden's grocery (centre) and Williams's tobacconist and stationer in the late 1940s, facing the Market Place, with a news placard announcing 'Cheaper Petrol'.

fate of the Tolpuddle Martyrs. They agreed that the six 'Dorchester Unionists' would be better off in the hulks and the colonies.

There was already a philosophical ocean between the prospective parson and the protesting peasantry. Barnes and Shrapnel were conservative Anglicans. The labourers from Tolpuddle were Nonconformist libertarians. Hence the military genius of the age was comfortable entertaining Barnes and they became close friends. Being fascinated with the mathematics of ballistics, Barnes credited to Shrapnel the 'proficiency in the exact sciences' which he intended bringing to his own meeker choice of subjects. Shrapnel explained the precise skills that were required by those of his ilk from young men who entered service with the British East India Company. Barnes saw this as the niche market for which his unique schooling methods could cater as he prepared to move back to Dorchester in 1836.

By this time, General Shrapnel had moved to Peartree House, beside Southampton Water, and Holbrook was the home of Henry Hall who was the master of a pack of hounds.

The greatest work of Wincanton plasterer George Day (1787–1858) collapsed with the demise of William Beckford's stupendous Fonthill Abbey. Beckford left for Bath in 1822 and Day returned to his home town. He lived in South Street, in what became Hartnell's Bakery, where his legacy was one of the finest examples of local craftsmanship. He moulded whirls and squares featuring grapes and acorns for the ceiling to his sitting-room beside the street. Appropriately, for what another Day turned into a bakery, it resembles icing decorating a wedding cake.

George Day also built the Baptist Church in Mill Street, in 1829, and became its unpaid pastor. Having founded its Sunday school he continued to spread what he described as 'ruling love' until incapacitated by blindness. After a lifetime working in the visible arts he was unable to come to terms with his disability.

The Grand Western Union Railway, to link Bath and Weymouth, was surveyed to the west of Wincanton, via Holbrook and Holton, by Roger Hopkins & Son in 1836. It would have crossed the Blackmore Vale and gone down the Cerne Valley to Dorchester but was one of the failures as the bubble of railway mania threatened to burst. In the event the first trains did not arrive for another two decades, with the Somerset Central Line in 1855, which became part of the Somerset and Dorset Railway.

West Hill House was built by parish Poor Law Overseer George Tompkins early in the nineteenth century. Coylton Terrace, overlooking the Blackmore Vale from Bayford Hill, was built by a Scotsman named Linton in the early 1830s. Hawker's Bridge at Southgate was built by Richard Stone, from Yarcombe, Devon, in 1833.

The Malthouse at Waterside was destroyed by fire on 3 July 1834. George Messiter, aged 58, died on 21 November 1834. Thomas Knighton was killed by a horse in 1835. In 1836, Uriah Coombes was run over and killed by a cart and John Gawler burnt to death. George Sweetman also records the destruction of Mr Cooper's new house by fire. It was a time of widespread change with Musgrave and Garrett's Bank closing, the first gaslights in the town being lit on 16 December 1836, and Wincanton and the West disappearing under 'mountains of snow' on 9 January 1837. Viscount Weymouth died at Shanks, Cucklington, and William IV was about to be committed to the vault under St George's Chapel at Windsor.

The National School, in North Street, was built in 1837. This was Queen Victoria's accession year – making it the earliest surviving Victorian building in Wincanton – and the project was under the auspices of the National Society for Promoting the Education of the Poor in the Principles of the Established Church. That was the snappy title given to Anglican elementary schools. Revd William Carpendale, who came to the parish in 1829, was its patron. He was 'consumed with zeal' but 'of delicate health', to quote George Sweetman, and died in August 1838. His widow, Emma, lasted for the remainder of the longest reign on record and died in Weymouth in January 1901 at the age of 91.

Carpendale had sermonised on the benefits to society of carrying out good deeds beyond the pulpit. This stance was echoed by his successor, Revd Henry Collins, to the continuing annoyance of James Baker who was churchwarden from 1840 to 1869. Baker was remembered as 'doom and gloom' for his pronouncements that priority should be given 'to the decaying fabric of the building' which he insisted was in an imminent state of collapse. He had one of the columns removed and replaced at his own expense. Later he saw the chancel arch torn out and it remained in pieces for years. Baker was 'out of heart with the whole businesses' but Collins stuck to his wider principles.

He had arrived as a curate and stepped into the breach before William Carpendale's death. Henry Collins expanded on his chosen text ('Who is sufficient for these things?') when he told his parishioners that like his predecessor he was going to concentrate on the welfare of children. He also laid down the ground rules for the adults:

I appear before you today in a situation of the very deepest responsibility – a minister accountable to God for upwards of 2,000 precious, never dying souls. This responsibility I feel more deeply today than I have since my coming among you, because I am now the minister and the sole minister of this parish.

The Union Workhouse, the Poor Law Institution for the district, dated from the Carpendale-Collins era. Unlike the brown Cornbrash limestone of the

Above: *Awnings and blinds concealing the shoes of Sydney Brock & Son* (left) *and ironmongery at Clementina* (right), *in the former home of the Messiter and Cash families, looking up the street from the sign of Moss Pharmacy in the summer of 2001.*

Left: *The imposing classical frontage of the White Horse Hotel with its pedimented porch, inscribed 'G.D. 1733' on the key-stone for George Deane.*

North side of the High Street in 2000 from the Bear Hotel, Sydney Brock & Son's shoe shop, offices at No. 5, and Mouton Messiter's grand eighteenth-century house, which is now Clementina ironmongers.

National School, its building material was brick, with some 200,000 being made of local Fuller's earth clay and fired on site, above the River Cale on the lower slope of West Hill. The foundation-stone was laid on 29 March 1837 and the project cost £3,550 with the main contractor being Davis of Langport. The transition between the old Poorhouse and new Workhouse was marked by the arrival of a foundling. Abandoned at South Gate Toll House, she was named Annie Southgate, and fostered by the newly appointed master and matron.

Church and town joined forces in Balsam Paddock to celebrate the coronation of Queen Victoria, with an 'immense parish festival' on 28 June 1838.

The popularity of Carpendale-Collins Anglicanism prompted a Nonconformist backlash. The National School in North Street backed on to the premises of the British School in Mill Street – with a high wall and barbed wire separating the two – with the educational wing of the Baptist Church, inspired by William Day, finding its master in F.R. Wood from the Toll House in the upper High Street. The two schools competed for pupils, at a penny per head per week, from 1837 until 1843 when the Wood family left Wincanton for Wiltshire. In the National School, Sweetman tells us, 'in Mr Fletcher's time the good old rule of 'whackem' was well kept up'.

George Wyndham succeeded General Shrapnel at Holbrook House. Colonel-Commandant of the Royal Artillery, Shrapnel was promoted Lieutenant-General, and received recognition for his invention, after leaving Wincanton. He had devised case-shot with bursting charges and bullets that turned high-explosive shells into fearful anti-personnel weapons. The Duke of Wellington testified to their effectiveness in 1808 but it was not until 1837 that General Shrapnel received a letter from Windsor Castle informing him of the King's readiness to confer a knighthood upon the inventor. King William IV then died and nothing more was heard of the proposal. General Shrapnel's last years were marred by this disappointment and he died at Peartree House, in Southampton, in 1842. He was buried in the family vault beneath the chancel of Bradford-on-Avon parish church in Wiltshire.

Charles Barton followed George Wyndham at Holbrook. Between 1846 and 1848 he extended the house and built a stable block and lodge. The location of the latter, on the roadside south of the house, shows that in late-Victorian times the entrance to the property, its driveway, was still from its historic location which was a little to the north-west of the modern roundabout.

It was an unfenced trackway which is shown on the first edition of the Ordnance Survey map, published in 1811, where it is depicted as starting to the north-west of Holbrook House, at Higher Holbrook. It then passed through the middle of the Holbrook House collection of buildings, to the east of

The lower High Street, eastwards from the roof of No. 5 Market Place, to the beech trees at Overton in the autumn of 2003.

the dovecote and between the main house and outbuildings that were removed in 1903. Until 1846 there was no lodge at the turnpike road and the trackway went straight across, still unfenced, over the fields to Stibbles Farm in the next valley and then beside the barns on Hungerhill and down into Higher Holton and Holton village.

Holbrook Lodge used to be dominated by a great range of four immense brick chimneys, built as a mock-Tudor flourish that was totally disproportionate to the size and needs of the tiny building and blamed for a continual damp problem. The lodge was locally known as 'Chimneys' until, after becoming unstable, they were removed in 1975. The lodge's former exaggerated look led Sir Nikolaus Pevsner to suggest it may have been the work of the architect Eden Nesfield (1835–88) who made a speciality of distinctive lodges and designed those at Kew Gardens and Hampton Court. Nesfield was only 27 when he engraved his *Specimens of Mediaeval Architecture in France and Italy* but regretfully it has to be admitted that there is no evidence that even he was producing lodges at the age of 11.

The Victorian grounds at Holbrook were to the south-west of the house, on either side of the present drive, where red chestnuts and mock oranges can still be seen. They extended to the site of the old kennels and a fine large Georgian-style carved-stone seat which is almost the length of a normal house.

The Trooper Club, which evolved into Wincanton Friendly Society, was established by veterans of the French Wars in 1842. Wincanton Coal Charity, dating from 1836, came into its own during the difficult decade that followed, and made arrangements with Somerset collieries to obtain supplies at wholesale prices. The railway brought easier availability and by the end of the century the 'Coal Club' was distributing between 50 and 70 tons a year, to more than 100 families, at an average price of 8s.4d. per ton (5d. a hundredweight).

New Victorian values saw the first shots in local resistance against 'the demon drink'. They were fired on 27 November 1843 with a public meeting to welcome and endorse the establishment of a National Temperance Society. It was to be a continuing fight for the rest of the century which united or divided congregations, families and the community in general. 'Nothing but te-te-total will do,' was the phrase of abstaining artisan Richard Turner from Preston in 1833. The word 'teetotaller' had entered the language with immediate effect.

Harry Burton, Romany's national King of the Gypsies, was taken ill at the roadside and died in Wincanton Union Workhouse at the age of 94 on 14 July 1847.

James Walters (1797–1848) seems to have lost his life during the revolution in France that resulted in the siege of Paris, during the rise of Louis Napoleon. This self-taught builder from Mill Street had been attached to the British Embassy there, a decade earlier in 1838, when he was librarian to the Episcopal bishop. He wrote passionate libertarian poems. Ill health caused him to return exhausted to Wincanton, where he recovered to give Shakespearean readings, but was then admitted to the Poor Law Institution for ten weeks in 1847. His friends raised funds to enable him to return to France but he arrived as the situation deteriorated and was there when the Archbishop of Paris was killed while tending the dying on 26 June 1848. James Walters was never heard of again.

A new stone pump and lamppost were erected beside the Shambles, in the Market Place, at a cost of £56.8s.4d. in 1848. George Sweetman records that the parish trustees contributed £40 towards the work, which was carried out by Wincanton Water Company, and that the pump stayed in place until Christmas 1879. In summer, when water was scarce, 'fighting for preference was often resorted to'. During the hard winters of Victorian times, things were even worse, 'when the footway was one block of ice'.

Years of work on establishing piped water and drainage systems can be credited to Thomas Richards who was born in 1812 at the former Roundhill Farmhouse. Having transformed hygiene and sanitation in the town, 'the greatest delight of his life' was doing away with 'the yoke of water-hauling'. He succeeded the late Herbert Messiter as chairman of the Feoffees of Town Charities in 1879. Mr and Mrs Richards were treated to a dinner in their honour at the Greyhound Hotel on 3 April 1887 to celebrate their golden wedding anniversary. It was provided by grateful residents and hosted by his 18-strong team of draughtsmen and labourers who presented a photographic album containing all their portraits.

George Green opened a public house on the south side of Bayford Hill. Originally the Rising Sun, in 1848, its name was changed to the Prince of Wales, probably after the young Prince Bertie had travelled through the town. Queen Victoria's accouchement, when 'Her Majesty was safely delivered of a prince,' to quote *The Times*, had taken place on 9 November 1841.

George Sweetman (1834–1917) lists in *The History of Wincanton* the public houses in the town, in the decade remembered as the Hungry Forties, beginning with those in Bayford:

I will include those at Bayford because they were supported by the townspeople, more than by the people of the hamlet. The White Horse at the top of the village street, The Crown in the centre, and The Unicorn at this end. Coming across the parish border-line were The Rising Sun near where The Prince of Wales now stands, The King's Arms where Mr Maddocks now lives, The Dolphin (Uncle Tom's Cabin had not been opened). Next came The Swan, where Mr Woodcock lives, then the White Horse, now Mr Deanesly's, The Bear Inn, where at the door the portly form of Host Grist could constantly be seen. The Greyhound kept by John Bayly, The Trooper where Mrs Slade lived, The Red Lion, occupied by Mr Joseph Hutchings, The White Hart in Church Street, The George in Mill Street, The Britannia in North Street, The Victoria in Tything, The New Inn in South Street.

Sweetman goes on to mention malthouses and breweries before observing:

No marvel that therefore that so many homes were wretched, and that the true welfare of the people was neglected. Sunday trade flourished, and in the villages around, at the public houses on the Lord's Day 'a roaring business' was done.

Wincanton Temperance Society had its roots in the activities of cobbler Jonathan Pardy and currier William Hart, who arranged for publicist James Teare to address a meeting, at the home of Dr Nathaniel Parsons in Mill Street, apparently in 1841. It was followed by a 'Pledge Book' opened by Benjamin Benjafield and James Sweetman on 2 September 1843. They were joined by Samuel Frost, as George Sweetman recalled with clarity from across the decades, by which time Benjafield had succumbed to the bottle:

On the 9th October, these young men met at my father's house at Shatterwell Shoots to sign the pledge for an indefinite period. They entered their names, left the book on the table, and went away to David Kiddle's Temperance Coffee House in Mill Street, to get some ginger beer to wet the contract. During their absence I wrote my name in their book, a piece of presumption for which I was chided on their return. They were annoyed that a boy under nine years of age should spoil their pledge book by putting in a name so soon, as they then thought, to be erased. To induce me to keep the pledge, Benjafield promised me a shilling on Xmas day if I remained true. He kept his promise, as I kept mine, and with the first shilling I ever had, I purchased a Universal Spelling Book, *and so laid the foundation of whatever education I have since had. Benjafield afterwards went to London, kept the tap* [tap-room beer bar] *at Charing Cross Hotel, and died there.*

Chaired by Henry Legg, with James Hannam as secretary, Henry French treasurer, and E. Walker its registrar, Wincanton Temperance Society modelled itself on a similar group already active in Gillingham. Lectures were held at the Town Hall, committee meetings in the Baptist schoolroom, and the inaugural 'Tea Meeting' on 23 January 1844. By the end of the year, playing on new year's eve, Wincanton Temperance Band was on the march. Its bandsmen were Aaron Bell, Benjamin Benjafield, William Edwards, John Gilbert, Ephraim Hobbs, John Horsey, Francis Kiddle, Richard King, and Uriah Pond.

The cause waxed and waned between gatherings of hundreds, outbreaks of apathy, and resistance ranging from derision to rotten eggs. The society was 'all but extinct' by August 1846 when Mr and Mrs George Royce arrived from Rutland and set about reviving it. By 1850 it was holding adult arithmetic and literary classes, in the evenings, at the National School. Andrew King opened his Temperance Coffee House and News Room in Clewett's Yard.

William Dupe, who was born in Stoney Stoke, became a centenarian in 1849.

Parties from Wincanton travelled by horse-drawn vans to Frome – the closest rail-head to the town in 1851 – to take the train to London for the Great Exhibition in the Crystal Palace. George Royce founded the Band of Hope in 1852. This was based at the National School and boasted a library of 300 'religious and self-help titles' which had been collected by William Pitman.

A chapel and concert hall in Lock's Lane at Wincanton was leased by Barney Giles in about 1855. He set about causing near riots, which ended with the building being demolished by its owners, after setting out to convert the town for the Mormonites. The Church of Jesus Christ of Latter Day Saints, founded by the visionary Joseph Smith and led on the ground by Brigham Young, had discovered their promised land in Salt Lake Valley, Utah, reached by a mass migration of pioneers on 24 July 1847. Wincanton Baptists were particularly outraged by Giles's advocacy and justification of polygamy which was not outlawed in the United States until 1882.

The County Police Station in North Street was built in 1856 and remained in use until 1973. Its normal staffing was an inspector, sergeant and constable. Wincanton Brass Band was re-formed in 1857, still under the auspices of the temperance movement, to lead a series of lively meetings that also attracted navvies as railway constructors approached Templecombe and Sherborne from Gillingham and Salisbury. The Wincanton bandsmen were:

William Pitman (Leader)
Silas Kiddle and Henry Meatyard (Cornets)
John Hannam and Charles Shawe (Saxhorns)
Aaron Bell (Trombone)
F. Shepperd (Piccolo)
Alfred King and Richard King (Ophicleide)
Jasmes Hill (drum)

In 1858, 12-year-old Charles Fletcher from Wincanton was talent-spotted by Lord Arundell and employed by him as vocalist and violinist at Wardour Castle. He went on to perform at St James's Hall. In 1869 he married a German pianiste whom he met while providing chamber music for the Countess of Ranfurly.

The Congregational Chapel in Mill Street throbbed with missionary activity after the arrival of Revd John Edwin Drover in 1847. His next imperative was to 'bring the church into the street' by removing the old cottages that hid it from public view. This was achieved in 1859, after their acquisition and demolition, with the building of the Congregational School Room, costing £600. It served as the British School for the town – the Nonconformist answer to the National School of the Anglicans – with additional rooms for infants being added in 1866 for £250. Pastor Drover also largely rebuilt the chapel, in 1862 for £840, and remained in post until the arrival of Revd James Houston in 1893. The Manse, the next building down the street, is now Orchard House.

Wincanton Wind Band was formed in 1860 and reformed into Wincanton Brass Band in 1890. The sound of brass has echoed across the decades and as Wincanton Silver Band it went on to celebrate a century and more of music-making in the town.

Uncle Tom's Cabin, the thatched cider house in the High Street, takes its name from the anti-slavery novel by Mrs Harriet Beecher Stowe (1811–96) who was the wife of Revd Calvin E. Stowe of Lane Theological Seminary in Cincinnati. *Uncle Tom's Cabin*, or *Life Among the Lowly*, was initially printed in serial form, in the *National Era* in 1851, and then published as a book in 1852. It made an enormous impact both home and abroad, hastening the outbreak of the American Civil War, and being translated into

23 languages. Negro suffering was highlighted for the first time, as far as a popular audience was concerned, with graphic descriptions of how husbands were separated from wives and the brutality of the regimes imposed by some slave owners. In her own words, Mrs Stowe had drawn together 'a collection and arrangement of real incidents' and presented them in order to achieve 'a general result'. Her period of popularity with the British was compromised in 1870 when in her next major writings she accused the poet Byron of having had an incestuous relationship with his half-sister. Such revelations outraged Victorian society.

Harriet Beecher Stowe's great admirer in Wincanton was Thomas Green who opened Uncle Tom's Cabin, in May 1861. It was the month that news arrived in Europe that the United States were rapidly disuniting. The first shots in the American Civil War were fired by Confederate General Gustave Toutant Beauregard on 12 April 1861. Things American were in vogue in Wincanton, where Barney Giles championed the Mormonites, and Thomas Green's adoption of the influential anti-slavery novel was a political statement in the other direction.

The Somerset and Dorset Railway began as an entirely Somerset affair when the first passenger train ran from Highbridge to Templecombe, in January 1862. The inaugural train along the remainder of the line, the Dorset Central Railway onward to Blandford, ran on 7 August 1863. In the other direction, for a whole generation, the whistle-blowing of the 07.10 service on arrival in Wincanton, en route to Bath, was the wake-up call for the town. 'Slow and Dirty' was fair enough as the nickname for the Somerset and Dorset Railway. Serious detractors preferred 'Slow and Doubtful' but devotees countered with 'Slow and Delightful' which summed up the situation simply and scenically. Stopping trains, for places like Wincanton, took nearly four hours to cover the length of the line.

Things were even worse at Templecombe, where through trains from Burnham-on-Sea to London had to reverse down the up-line of the main line LSWR track from Exeter, in order to reach the high-level platform for the next stage of the journey. These manoeuvrings inspired the following ditty:

In Wessex did you keep slow company
With the 'tanks' (royal) of the S and D,
That waited, as it seemed, for the crack of doom
While they performed strange rites at Templecombe.

Wincanton Station retained original quadrant signals with wooden arms for a century. In other respects it was ahead of its time, being one of the first stations in Somerset to be lit by gas, and the bridges southwards from Cole are the red-brick arches typical of the Dorset Central section rather than being stone-built arches characteristic of Somerset proper. An attractive stone arch was built in 1865 to cover the public well and fountain at Shatterwell Shoots. The Wilts and Dorset Bank opened a Wincanton branch.

The population streamed into the streets on the night of 17 November 1866 as the 'Great Meteor Shower' hit the atmosphere. What would have been regarded as an ill omen by previous generations could now be explained by science. The Leonid projectiles – named for the constellation marking their direction of approach – are an annual occurrence but vary in apparent intensity according to time and visibility. Sky watchers in Wincanton claimed a total of 1,265 meteorites in four hours.

The Market House and Town Hall were greatly extended in 1867 at a cost of £800. Tom Rogers founded a drama company which produced its first plays in 1871.

The campaign against the demon drink resumed its salvationist roll. Delicensed in 1871, the Trooper Inn on the south side of Church Street was chosen by James Sweetman for his Coffee Tavern and Temperance Hotel. An entirely new building, in neat red brick, replaced the rustic Trooper on the site in 1878.

The Union Workhouse below West Hill, was also expanded in 1871, at a cost of £2,000, into an enormous barrack-like Victorian structure. An infirmary was built beside it. Further rooms were added in 1901 when it catered for 250 inmates drawn from the town and surrounding villages.

Hillside and Wassall House, on Bayford Hill, were built in 1872. So too was the Masonic Hall in South Street, which opened on 13 June 1872, and work started on the Wesleyan Chapel which opened in 1873. Turnpike road tariffs were abolished in 1874 and Somerset's varied collection of toll-houses, including those in and around Wincanton, became private homes. After the dismantling of its iron gate, the frontage of that on the corner of the upper High Street with Common Road had its porch removed, in order to widen the highway.

Wincanton had two centenarians around this time. The first was Mrs Isabella Sly, in 1873. Having retired from Malkin Hill Farm, more than half a century earlier in January 1822, she died on 9 December 1875 at the age of 102. The next was labourer Noah Atkins but he barely survived his great day and died on 18 December 1881 at the age of 100.

The Wincanton Brewery, owned by Charles Child, stood between the National School and No. 11 North Street. Now with a flat roof, the three-storey extension at the rear was built as the maltster's premises, in about 1875. Advertisements for 'Pale and Old Ale, Stout and Porter' feature what would have been a very modern locomotive in the background, on the Somerset and Dorset Railway, although in appearance it resembles George Stephenson's *Rocket*. Once all trains must have looked like this.

The railway suffered a serious operational setback on 26 February 1877 when Midland Railway 0-4-4T tank engine No. 1282 derailed near Wincanton. Its driver was killed. The accident was blamed on an incompatibility between the engine type and the layout of the track. Similar engines had to stop at Evercreech until the rails were eventually re-laid through Wincanton.

A total of 20 dilapidated cottages were demolished in a clearance scheme in Grant's Lane in 1876. The old Market House and its adjacent lock-up, known locally as the 'Roundhouse' or blind-house', were destroyed by fire at midnight on 9 August 1877. The buildings were replaced by the present red-brick Town Hall, with a clock tower, in 1878. The architect was Willcocks of Bath who also rebuilt Horsington church. His effort on behalf of Wincanton brought a frown to architectural historian Sir Nikolaus Pevsner who dismissed the Town Hall as 'rather an eyesore with its ugly turret'. Functionality also removed a traffic obstacle by realigning the building with adjoining frontages. The opening ceremony took place on 23 October 1878 and the Shambles was removed on 27 November 1879.

The Town Hall clock was installed by Gillet and Brand of Croydon in 1878 and cost a total of £72.3s.5d. for the mechanism and its east and west faces. The north face was added later. Time changed for the nation and the world as a result of the Geodetic Congress in Rome, in October 1883, and the ratification of Greenwich as 'the universal meridian' by an international conference in Washington which took place a year later. The location of Wincanton is around latitude 51 degrees four minutes north and longitude two degrees 25 minutes west (which is for a point a few metres from the finishing post at the present-day Wincanton Racecourse).

The wider implications were that travellers inside time zones no longer had to adjust their watches. Time, for Wincanton, went forward by nearly ten minutes in adopting London standard time. To be precise, in the unlikely event of self-calibration resuming popularity, true sun time in Wincanton is nine minutes 40 seconds after Greenwich Mean Time and 51 minutes 20 seconds ahead of British Summer Time. That once took me an afternoon to work out, back in 1987, and the mathematics still baffle me.

Henry Messiter died on 9 October 1879 at the age of 76 and Herbert Messiter followed him later in the month, aged 38. Henry's widow, Susan Ellen Messiter, left Wincanton for Kensington, where she died on 18 November 1900 at the age of 82.

The greatest snowfall of the century brought Wincanton and the entire West Country to a standstill on 18 January 1881.

Until 1881, Catholics from Wincanton such as Italian trader Thomas Clementina and Anglican convert Captain John Bradney of Bayford Lodge walked or rode to Mass at Bonham, near Stourton. Father Ambrose Cotham was the priest at Bonham. His brother, Father William Cotham, came to Wincanton to say the Mass in Thomas Clementina's house in North Street on the last Sunday in May 1881. Clementina then gave £500 towards the buying of Acorn House, South Street, for a mission to the town which was inaugurated on 18 October 1881.

Abbot Gasquet and his Benedictines from Downside Abbey officiated on the Feast of St Luke in 1881. They were joined by Franciscans from Clevedon but handed over the following year to discalced (shoeless) Carmelites from Kensington Square, on 21 December 1882, with the consecration of what was only the second Priory to be established in England since the Reformation. It was under Father Edmund Sharples.

The New Jerusalem Church founded a Wincanton branch in 1882. It met on Sundays in the Good Templars' Hall. Followers were generally known as Swedenborgians, having adopted the work of the theologian Emanuel Swedenborg (1688–1772), which was institutionalised as a sect. They believed that Swedenborg, who came to London from Stockholm, had experienced both heaven and hell and that the Last Judgment and Second Coming had taken place during his lifetime. The church found new disciples across the country as it prepared to celebrate its centenary in London on 13 August 1883.

Locally, the first organised shots in what was now the national game, were bowled on the flat top of Old Hill by Wincanton Cricket Club in 1883. Wincanton Fire Brigade was established in 1886 under the captaincy of William Theodore Goodfellow from the Greyhound Hotel. He could muster a dozen men to bring the horse-drawn appliance out of the engine house in Mill Street.

The parish churchyard saw its last burials in 1886, leading George Sweetman to calculate how many 'mute inglorious Miltons' had been buried in its 3,170 square yards:

Taking the average burials per annum as 25, from 1313 to 1886, when the graveyard was closed, we have 14,325. We have at least six burials in every grave. Their only record is the parish register, and those only since 1636. What a blow to the vanity of those who would lord it over the soil and over their fellows, during their short period here!

The Carmelite Priory, behind Acorn House, was designed by diocesan architect Canon A. J. Scoles in 1887. The foundation-stone of 'the new Monastery' was laid on 16 July 1888 and it was completed on 18 August 1889. It was dedicated to St Luke.

Apostolic fervour set the priests off to Sherborne and Yeovil where they said the Mass in private houses but in 1891 the Superior General of the Order issued a directive that they were to return to Wincanton. Nuns arrived in the town, down the slope in the last house between North Street and Shatterwell, where the Convent of St Joseph was established by the Ursuline Sisters of Jesus in 1892.

The state of the parish church had long been a cause for concern. Back in the 1840s, churchwarden John Baker had personally intervened to pay to restore some of the columns, but the chancel arch remained unstable and had to be removed. Four decades later, Victorian aspirations and wealth were causing the restoration or rebuilding of medieval churches across the land, and it became an embarrassment that Wincanton was being left behind. The galleries were regarded as old fashioned, walls were damp, and even attempts at heating left the old flagstone floor awash with condensation. Revd Richard Nicolson, who arrived as rector in 1884, set about obtaining architectural reports and threw his energies into convincing the community that there was only one option. Then Nicholson died, in 1885, which ironically gave the unstarted project a boost by bringing pledges and promises to turn it into his lasting memorial.

Rebuilding, at a cost of £6,000 largely funded by Miss Chafyn Grove, began in 1887 and was completed and consecrated on 15 August 1889. The designs were by London architect J.D. Sedding. Only the fourteenth-century embattled tower remained from the original building, now at the end of the north aisle rather than the nave, which had moved southwards across the former south aisle as that in turn moved towards the churchyard. The next rector, Revd Colin Grant-Dalton (1860–98), could boast a church that seated 700 on its oak benches.

Two recreational milestones date from this time. Revd James Bennett, from South Cadbury, and High Street bookseller George Sweetman founded Wincanton Field Club, in June 1889, for outdoor meetings to introduce a wider public to antiquarian and natural history studies. Among those who gave lectures – on 'Water and Waterspouts' – was the Congregational parson, geology teacher and professor of mathematics Dr George Deane (1837–91) from Spring Hill Cottage. Although born in Wells he came from the Deane family of Wincanton drapers, who established the business that became New and Morgan, in South Street. Younger elements in the community responded to the enthusiasm for the natural sciences by forming Wincanton Football Club in 1890.

Vaccination has pricked raw nerves in recent times which is hardly surprising as television reports have brought into our homes the grotesque evidence of brain damage allegedly caused against all the odds to children who might have done better to catch whooping cough. If, despite the arguments on both sides, modern parents find it tough to rationalise a decision, then imagine the potential *cause célèbre* you would have if vaccination were made compulsory.

It used to be. Parliament passed the law in 1863, to bring smallpox under control, and in so doing it brought medical ethics to the forefront of political debate. In 1870 the Anti-Vaccination Society was formed and in 1885 Leicester saw one of the greatest protest demonstrations ever held in Britain, in protest to an enforcement campaign that had led to many being fined.

The argument also woke up Wincanton and raged into the 1890s. In particular it seems to have split the Rutter family if, as I take it, Clarence Edwin Rutter and 'T.E.R.' came from the same stable. They both wrote as if they were solicitors. Clarence resorted to the broadsheet, a traditional form of English protest, to make the case against vaccination on 26 June 1894:

This operation I am ordered to have performed under the authority of Acts of Parliament, backed up by strong medical opinion. Of course it is easy to obey, but I feel my responsibility as a parent. My child is well and healthy, and the whole thing seems so unnatural and repulsive to me, that I cannot assent to it, unless there is an urgent need for its being performed. I therefore enquire again more closely, and am told it is not an absolute preventive, that it needs to be done again and again, but that if it does not absolutely prevent small-pox, it will make any attack much more slight. This appears to me to take away more than half the supposed advantage. I find further that authorities differ, that whole districts and towns are practically unvaccinated, and that in spite of prophesies to the contrary, there is no more smallpox there than in well vaccinated places. That shakes my belief in vaccination sadly. I hear too of children injured by it, and experienced mothers who call it a wicked and cruel law.

He went on to question 'whether the State has any more business to enforce a medical belief, than it once had to enforce a religious one.' Clarence Rutter urged 'both the Board and the Bench' – namely the Board of Guardians and Bench of Magistrates – to observe 'the conscientious objection of parents' and 'realise what an odious and tyrannical thing it is to prosecute their neighbours'. He did not pull his punches. 'Give up these prosecutions,' he demanded.

This was dangerous ground for a solicitor. However, T.E.R.'s answer of 6 July 1894 concentrated on the tribal benefits that had been seen to result from a programme of vaccination. He argued that individual freedom cannot extend to a right to deprive one's children of protection because of 'foolish whims and fancies':

Such conduct seems both unparental and unpatriotic. It not only does a wrong to their own unfortunate children, but is most unfair to the law-abiding majority, who adopt the legal remedy under the reasonable hope that, by its universal application, the terrible plague of smallpox may in the course of a few years be absolutely exterminated within these islands.

His pamphlet, entitled *The Anti-Vaccination Craze: A Counter-blast*, goes on to conclude with a powerful

THE NINETEENTH CENTURY

The High Street upwards from Uncle Tom's Cabin (left) being decked out with flags and spruce trees, and a banner 'God bless Victoria' for the Queen's diamond jubilee in 1897.

Above: Boys and girls from the Anglican Sunday school put out the flags twice in 1897 – for the Queen's birthday and for her diamond jubilee celebrations later in the year.

Inset: Cast-iron plaque on one of the jubilee seats which graced Wincanton to mark the achievement of the longest reign on record and its sixtieth anniversary in 1897.

Wincanton Town Band assembling to mark Queen Victoria's diamond jubilee in 1897.

Captain Pratt from Chichester brought the Church Army's 'No. 1 Van' to Balsam Paddock in May 1899 at the invitation of South Street draper Henry Snook.

punch below the belt though the effect was spoilt by a sentence that is impossibly verbose:

As Mr Clarence E. Rutter avails himself of this opportunity to trot out for our edification the rather stale and hackneyed 'Nonconformist conscience', it may be respectfully suggested to those who, upon principle (whether they believe in vaccination or not) deem it in their duty to disobey the law, that they would be acting a much more patriotic part, and doing far greater honour to what they are pleased to call their 'conscience', if during the pressure of this 'wicked and cruel law', they were simply to refrain altogether for a season from the procreation of children, until the object of the Legislature shall have been attained by the extinction of the disease, and this temporary tyranny of the parliamentary lancet be overpast.

In unravelling the meaning behind the injunction to refrain 'for a season from the procreation of children' one has to think laterally of a suitable pun. The dictionary may help with a definition of the root word, to 'rut', which is usually associated with stags. In other words, Mr Rutter, stop rutting.

When Wincanton Racecourse appeared in *The Racing and Dramatic News*, such as its detailed entry on 28 February 1891, it was for the old course to the south-east of Anchor Hill at Hatherleigh Farm. That particular day was for a straight point-to-point meeting rather than an oval steeplechase course. The occasion was something like a miniature version of the Glastonbury Festival, in that tents, stalls and the grandstand were re-erected each year, along with a field telephone system with 18 poles set up for the benefit of officials, stewards and the police.

St Joseph's, a Catholic school down the hill in North Street, was founded by the Ursuline Sisters in 1892. With an average roll of 37 it could cater for up to 60 children. The nuns lived in adjoining Rockhill House and the two buildings were linked by a subway.

Adopting Grand National rules, Wincanton Hunt Steeplechases became the first such events in the land, with the first meeting taking place at Hatherleigh Racecourse, Lattiford, on Easter Monday in 1893. J. Martin Richards, on Princess, won the Cheriton Stakes there on 3 April 1893. His son, Nathan Richards, and grandson Sir Gordon Richards (1904–86), kept up the tradition. The latter's 4,870 winners famously included local horse Wicked Uncle from Little Weston, near Sutton Montis.

Two Victorian ladies view portraits in the window of photographer Edward Goodfellow at No. 47 High Street, next to coal agent Thomas Budgen and thatched Uncle Tom's Cabin beside the entrance to Flinger's Lane, c.1885.

The town's Ford dealers, Thomas Budgen & Son, turned No. 33 High Street into the Ireson Garage in 1917 and remained for nearly half a century.

Cullingford Carpets (left) *and the old Post Office at No. 20 High Street* (centre), *which closed in 1974, and a ladder propped against No. 18, on a quiet day in 1984.*

Chapter Five
Shops and Trades

Early closing of shops, beginning after lunch at two o'clock on Thursday afternoons, was introduced in 1893:

Following the example of many other towns, instead of waiting for implementation on the matter of early closing, Wincanton tradesmen have unanimously agreed to adopt the weekly half-holiday system. They have some time closed at four o'clock, and the holiday has been appreciated by both employer and employed. They have now unanimously decided to close on Thursdays at two o'clock, the banks closing at one o'clock. It is hoped the public will assist this movement, so that the arrangement having been made it may be fully carried out. Early closing will commence on Thursday 6 April.

George Sweetman's *Wincanton Street and Trade Directory* of 1894 gives a fascinating snapshot of the town which comes into clear focus through his detailed descriptions of their locations. This, together with *Kelly's Directory* and large-scale Ordnance Survey maps, enables us to travel back in time and re-walk the late-Victorian streets. Although Sweetman recorded the results of the first attempt at introducing street numbering, in 1886, he was uneasy with the concept of odd numbers for one side of the road and even numbers on the other, and would have preferred consecutive numbering instead. The town's basic skeleton remains as it was in 1894:

<u>The Batch</u>

Rodber House, H. Gulley
Wincanton Union Workhouse (John Barnes, master)
Mrs William Warren
Mrs Samuel Richards
Harry Smart (Insurance agent)
Wallace Withers (Porter, Somerset and Dorset Railway)
Samuel Sweetman (Mason)
Hubert Cross
James Durrant
Nursery Cottage, Mrs James Sweetman
Mrs Hannam
Mrs Hinks

<u>Bayford Hill (north side, upwards and eastwards)</u>

No. 1 Coylton Terrace (initially known as Ireson Villas), Mrs Adney
No. 3 Coylton Terrace (also known as Ireson Villas), George Richards (Auctioneer)
No. 5 Coylton Terrace, Ladies' School (Miss Loader, principal)
No. 7 Coylton Terrace, John Hannam (Gentleman)
No. 9 Coylton Terrace, George Washbourne (County Court Clerk)
Nos 11 and 13 Coylton Terrace, John Hannam (Grocer; private residence)
No. 15, Miss Day
No. 17, South Bank, William Bailey Langhorne JP
No. 19, John Wilcox
No. 21, Thomas White

<u>Bayford Hill (south side, eastwards)</u>

No. 2, East Gate House
No. 4, Arthur Yells (Brewer's agent)
No. 6, Hillside, Mrs McKay
No. 8, Mrs Andrew Thomas
No. 10, George Ford
No. 12, Henry Feltham
No. 14, Louis Warren
No. 16, John Spearing
No. 18, Robert Humphries (Mason)
No. 20, Samuel Benjafield
No. 22, James Burgess
No. 24, Prince of Wales Inn (Mr Davidge, landlord)
No. 25, Walter Drew (Gardener)
No. 28, Alfred Laver
No. 30, Mrs Williams
No. 32, Rose Cottage, Miss Eda Feltham (Dressmaker)
No. 34, William Read (Gentleman)
No. 36, George Read (Solicitor's clerk)

<u>Church Street (south side, downwards from the east)</u>

No.1 (empty)
Nos 3–5, William Newman (Tinman and ironmonger)
No. 7, Frank Sweetman (Mason)

Pills and tobacco on sale in Ebenezer Carrington's drug store at No. 23 High Street, in c.1904 with a poster for the Palestine Exhibition (left centre) in the Assembly Rooms, Bath, beside the alleyway into Lock's Lane.

Changes continue in 1989, uphill from Carrington Way (left) *with the Cheltenham & Gloucester Building Society offices for sale, next to Banks the Chemist and the entrance to the new Camelot Centre* (left arch), *beside Wincanton News.*

Left: *Edwin Dowding's grocery sign at No. 45 High Street with one of the earliest motorcycle combinations and two prams behind the sidecar* (centre), *opposite the Dolphin Hotel* (right), *c.1905.*

The wide part of the High Street, down from No. 44 (left, demolished in 1959 for the entrance to a car park) *and the Old Manse at No. 57* (right) *down to the sign of the Dolphin Hotel and the blind of grocer Edwin Dowding, beside the studio of photographer Edwin Goodfellow, c.1910.*

SHOPS & TRADES

Making a political statement by adopting the title of Harriet Beecher Stowe's anti-slavery novel, Uncle Tom's Cabin was named by Thomas Green at the start of the American Civil War, in May 1861.

The entrance into the new Carrington Way in 1984, with Take Four outfitters (left) and Gillam's Car Spares (centre), in former outbuildings behind the High Street.

No. 4, Baptist School Rooms
Baptist Chapel
No. 6, Mrs Richard King
No. 8, Miss Cross (Tailoress), Mrs Alfred King and Alfred Stacey
No. 10, Henry Stacey (Cooper)
No. 12, Mrs Richard King
No. 14, Robert John Beaton (Tailor), Henry Day (Mason), Charles Newport, Mrs Maber, Mrs Ashford and Mrs Mills
Congregational Chapel
No. 16, Board School (Mr Hoyle, master)
No. 18, The Manse (Revd John Edwin Drover)
No. 20, William Horn
No. 22, Charles Rawlings
No. 24, Mrs Charles Harvey (Furniture dealer)
No. 26, James Player (Bootmaker)
No. 28, William Dymond (Bootmaker)
Gap: George Inn Yard
   George Inn (William Rex, landlord)

Moor Lane

Robert Thompson
Mrs Foote
No. 25, South Gate House, William Roper (Chimney-sweep)
No. 26, William Day
No. 27, Mrs Benjamin Read
No. 28, George Everett
No. 29, John Smart
No. 30, Mr Hexter (Signalman)
No. 31, Lawrence House, James Henry Lippiatt (Farmer)

North Street (west side, northwards)

No. 1 (Empty)
National School (Board School, girls and infants)
Wincanton Brewery

Nos 5–7, Thomas Clementina (Merchant)
No. 9, Henry Cox (Basketmaker)
No. 11, John Pound
No. 13, Henry Meatyard (Smith)
No. 15 (Empty)
No. 17, Joseph Cave (Shopkeeper)
No. 19, Mrs Mitchell
Wesleyan Chapel
St Joseph's (Roman Catholic School)

North Street (east side, northwards)

No. 2, J.C. Hinks (Draper)
No. 4, William Evans (Bootmaker)
No. 6, Herbert Evans (Bootmaker)
No. 8, Mrs John Symes (Veterinary surgeon)
No. 10, Miss Chamberlain
No. 12, Edwin Couch and Walter William Harris (Rates collector and photographer)
No. 14, Mrs John Baily
No. 16, George Reakes
No. 18, Mrs Whitaker
No. 20, Police Station (Superintendent J. Williams and Sergeant Fairchild)

Shatterwell

No. 1, Charles Cross
No. 2, Samuel Laver
No. 3, Mrs Tucker (Laundress)
No. 4, Mrs Cox (Laundress)
No. 5, Shatterwell House, Stephen Roberts
No. 6, Thomas Woodcock
No. 7, Samuel Hiscock
No. 8, William Tanswell
No. 9, Joseph Parsons
No. 10, Mrs English
No. 11 Bath Terrace, Mrs Thomas
No. 12 Bath Terrace, Alfred Wadman
No. 13 Bath Terrace, George Dashwood

Car, lorry and carts in the 1920s, westwards down from the 1918-built Methodist Church (left) *and the Dolphin Hotel.*

Eastwards, to Bayford Hill, along the north side of the High Street from Nos 69 and 71 (left) *and the gates of Pear Tree House in 1900, then Nos 73 to 83* (centre) *with trees obscuring Ireson Villas and Coylton Terrace.*

✦ SHOPS & TRADES ✦

'Teas' at No. 48 (left) facing the signs for the Guest Tea House in No. 61 above Uncle Tom's Cabin (behind PK 1827) in 1935.

The Toll House (left) from the west, across to ladders and workmen at No. 81 (Stonecroft) next to No. 83 High Street and the entrance to Ireson Lane beside the wall below Ireson Villas.

The Cattle Market in Station Road, north-westwards to the parish church (top right), *in 1909.*

John Bartlett's butchers, in their original location at No. 7 Market Place, at Christmas in 1895.

SHOPS & TRADES

A motorcycle with tricycle attachment, c.1910, outside Edward Spencer's jewellers in No. 3 High Street.

Christmas holly bedecking Billy Loud's butchers, at what is now the entrance to Carrington Way, in about 1920.

Eight carts stacked around the arched entrance to the Dolphin Hotel, in c.1885 when Charles Howes was the landlord, facing the projecting sign for Uncle Tom's Cabin (right).

Silver Street (west side, northwards)

No. 1, George Acutt (Commercial traveller)
No. 3, W.E. Keefe (Solicitor)
No. 5, Thomas Johnson (Refreshment rooms)
No. 7, Mrs Cross
Gap: Richmond Place
   No. 1, Mrs Ashfield. No. 2, Mrs William Winter. No. 3, Mrs Peter Dove. No. 4, Mrs Parsons. No. 5, Edwin Deane (Pedlar). No. 6, Albin Wadman. No. 7, Mrs Richard Vallis. No. 8, Mrs Abednego Benjafield. No. 9, William Parsons (Shoemaker). No. 10, Henry Hinks (Working engineer). No. 11, Charles Cook. No. 12, Charles Hole (Tailor). No. 13, Henry Targett (Barber)
No. 9 Silver Street, John Stringfellow
No. 11, Mrs Sopia Dowding
No. 13, Albert Clewett
No. 15, John Light
No. 17, Joseph Nut
No. 19, William Churchey
No. 21, Mrs George Paul
No. 23, James Butt (Van driver for Somerset and Dorset Railway)

Silver Street (east side, northwards)

No. 2, Albert Serrell (Grocer)
No. 4, Johnston's Stores
No. 6, Serrell's Stores
No. 8, Player's Stores
No. 10, Butt's Stores
No. 12, Mrs William Bond
No. 14, William Marks (Signalman)
No. 16, Charles Sims (Tailor)
No. 18, Glove Factory
No. 20, John Cairns
No. 22, E.G. Plomer (Horse-breaker)

South Street (west side, from the Town Hall)

No. 2, Hannam's Grocery (William Hannam, proprietor)
No. 4, John Gibbs (Baker)
No. 6, Harry Young (Saddler)
No. 8, Charles Pocock (Florist and seedsman)
No. 10, New Inn (John Parsons, landlord)
No. 12, Edward Yalden Cooper (Solicitor)
No. 14, Miss Stutfield
No. 16, John Thomas (Mason)
No. 18, William T. Goodfellow (Coach builder)
No. 20, Mrs Vallis (Dressmaker)
No. 22, Goodfellow's Coach Manufactory
No. 24, The Dogs, Mrs B. Bracher

South Street (east side, from the Market Place)

No. 1, Edward J. New (Draper)
No. 3, Walter Valder Gates (Private residence)
No. 5, Stuckey's Bank (F. Thirwall Fowler, manager)
No. 7, New Inn Yard
No. 9, William Edward Cooper (Solicitors)
No. 11, Walter March (Smith)
No. 13, St Luke's Catholic Church (Revd. Father Colin Sebastian)
No. 15, The Priory of St Luke and St Teresa (Revd Father Bernard Brun and Revd Father Aloysius Coghlan)
No. 17, Peter Bovenizar
No. 19, Archibald Ford (Rural postman)
No. 21, Mrs Woods
No. 23, John Grinter (Tailor)
No. 25, Tout Hill House, Count de la Pasture

Station Road

No. 1, Refreshment Rooms (William Rex)
No. 2, Matthew William Pickford (Draper)
No. 3, John Thomas (Station Master)
No. 4, Ferderick Francis (Tailor)
No. 5, Edwin Gifford
No. 6, Henry Dyke (Coal merchant)
No. 7, F. Dowding
No. 8, Revd Walter Farrer (Curate) and Fredrick Tucker (Sexton)

Carts in 1895, from the terrace at Nos 62 to 56 (left) across to No. 71, the gate leading to Pear Tree Close, No. 73, and the figure approaching No. 75 (right).

SHOPS & TRADES

Left: *Brian Dite's licensed betting office at No. 46 (right), and the Restaurant Café on the south side of the upper High Street, in 1984.*

Below: *The stone-built terrace above the Dolphin Hotel (left) and Johnson's Fruit Shop down to David and Penny Newlove Antiques and the Wincanton Bread Shop (right) in December 1984.*

No. 9, George Ford (Gardener) and J.W.G. Hathaway (Organist)
No. 10, Wincanton Railway Station
No. 11, Taunton & Company's Milk Depot (F. Dowding, manager)
No. 12, Wincanton Coal Gas Limited
No. 13, Gas Works House (Uriah Lewis, manager)
No. 14, John J. Granger (Tailor)
No. 15, Rose Cottage, Mrs Daw (Laundress)
No. 16, Mrs James Clewett
No. 17, Railway Inn (James Atkins Hill, landlord)
No. 18, Mrs Peters
No. 19, Alfred Jordan (Chimney-sweep)
No. 20, Mrs J. Parsons (Shopkeeper)
No. 21, Mrs James Meares
No. 23, Mrs Coombs
No. 24, Mr Green (Carpenter)
No. 25, Harry Feltham (Carpenter)
No. 26, William Willis
No. 27, Charlotte Davidge
No. 28, Mr Henning (Agent for Blackie and Company)
No. 29, Robert Meares
No. 30, Charles Riddick (Labourer)
No. 31, George Doman
No. 32, William Foyle (Labourer)
No. 34, Charles Davidge (Labourer)
No. 35, Tom Rice (Groom)
No. 36, Elizabeth Davidge
Nos 37 and 38, Thomas Huss (Bailiff)

Thornwell Lane

Nos 5–6, in ruins
No. 7, Mrs Walters
No. 8, Alphonso Oborn

No. 9, James Hutchings
No. 10, Thomas Viner
No. 11, Edward Perrett (Blacksmith)
No. 12, Bedford Place, Frank Sweetman (Mason)
No. 13, Bedford Place, John Long (Insurance agent)
No. 14, Life Guards Villas (Miss Sandison)
No. 15, John William Eden (Grocer; private residence)
No. 16, Frank Tucker
No. 17, Harry Turner (Rural postman)
No. 18, Robert Snook (Plasterer)
No. 19, John Prankard
No. 20, Alfred Thick
No. 21, Thomas Edwards (Mason)
No. 22, Miss Foot (Dressmaker)
No. 23 (Empty)
No. 24, Mrs Coles

Tything (east side, down from Tout Hill House)

No. 1, Mrs William Bracher
No. 2, Thomas Hudson (Auctioneer and architect)
No. 3, Susan Cox (Cane-seat worker)
No. 4, David Smith (retired Police Sergeant)

Tything (west side, down from Tout Hill)

No. 1, George Cox (Common lodging-house)
No. 2, Pound House, P. Bowering
No. 3, William Butt
No. 4, Mary Ann Atkins (Shopkeeper)
No. 5, James Bacon
No. 6, Newton Villas, W.J. Dyke (Relieving Officer)
No. 7, Thomas Sheppard
No. 8, Carmel Villa, Richard Henry Hoyle (Schoolmaster)
No. 9, Samuel Burgess (Railway inspector) and Revd James Houston (Congregational minister)
No. 1 Priory Villas (Empty)
No. 2 Priory Villas, Mrs Truscott (Dressmaker)

Downhill from Wincanton Café (left) *and the Gift and China Shop to Uncle Tom's Cabin and the blinds and shop fronts above Ireson Garage* (centre left) *in the 1960s.*

The Prince of Wales public house in about 1905, when George Robert Sweetman was publican, looking westwards to Hillside House and Wassall House (centre).

SHOPS & TRADES

No. 3 Priory Villas, Joseph Scadding (Under Bailiff to County Court)
No. 4, Priory Villas, Samuel Shaw (Colporteur)
No. 5 Priory Villas, Mrs Edwin Hutchings
No. 6 Priory Villas (Empty)
Bellfield House, Surrey Central Dairy Company (Walter Valder Gates, manager)

Verrington

Cutts Close, Edwin Plomer (Farmer)
Verrington, William Perry
Verrington, James Cannon
Verrington Lane, James Seager (Mason)
Verrington Lane, Jeremiah Morris (Labourer)

Waterside (off North Street)

No. 1, B. Wilmott
No. 2, George Bargery
No. 3 (Empty)
No. 4, Stephen Wright (Butcher)

West Hill (also known as Tompkin's Hill)

Frederick William Lancaster (Clerk to Guardians of Rural Sanitary Authority, School Attendance Committee, Highway and School Boards, and Superintendent Registrar and Vaccination Officer)
West Hill House, Mrs C.J. Shaw
Pencader House (empty)
The Mount, Mrs S.H. Longman
Sampson Bamford (Gentleman)
Sudden Grange, S.U. Martin
Sudden Farm, Joseph Sims
Holbrook House, Charles Barton J.P.
Holbrook Farm, William Herridge
New Barn, Mr Parker

Whitehall Cottages (below North Street)

Nos 1 and 2, Jesse Mitchell (Mason)
No. 3, Joseph Jacobs
No. 4, Frank Helliar
No. 5, William Morris
No. 6, James Gratewood
No. 7, Charles Lucas
No. 8, Frank Trim
No. 9, William Pocock
No. 10, Mrs Hansford
No. 11, Albert Haskett
No. 12, George Edwards
No. 13, William B. Feltham
No. 14 (Empty)

No, 15, James Rumble
No. 16, William Clements
No. 17, Harry Burge
Nos 18 and 19, John Warren
No. 20, Robert Rumble
No. 21, William Spearing

The young rector who supervised the restoration and rebuilding of the parish church, Revd Colin Grant-Dalton who was appointed in 1885, became chronically ill and was forced to resign. The curate, Revd Walter Farrer, took his place in 1896. This was in time for the diamond jubilee, of Queen Victoria, due to be celebrated as 'the longest reign on record'. The precise moment of the anniversary of the accession was at 2.20a.m. on 20 June 1897 but, this being a Sunday, the British Empire's week-long show of thanksgiving began the following day. 'From my heart, I thank my beloved people,' were the Queen's words, telegraphed around the globe, as she touched a button in Buckingham Palace. Grant-Dalton prayed 'for a few more years yet' for both the monarch and himself – granted in the case of the 78-year-old Queen – but the 38-year-old clergyman died on 31 January 1898.

The lasting mark of Queen Victoria's diamond jubilee celebrations was a series of commemorative seats erected around the town in the summer of 1897. A longer era had ended on 14 January 1897 with the death at the age of 87 of William Churchey. He was the last of the distinguished family that had been associated with Wincanton for four centuries.

The Elementary School in South Street had opened on 17 December 1896. The architect was Thomas Hudson and the builder Thomas Green. Its opening ceremony was conducted by the Right Honourable Henry Hobhouse MP from Hadspen House who was a member of the Royal Commission on Secondary Education. The buildings cost £4,600 and could accommodate 160 boys, 160 girls and 140 infants, although the average attendance was 103 boys, 90 girls and 60 infants. The master was Richard Henry Hoyle, with Miss Hacker the mistress, and Miss E. Richardson the infants' mistress.

Of the 169 inmates in Wincanton Union Workhouse in the summer of 1898, according to George Sweetman, the majority were of advanced years:

82 of them were above 60 years of age, and the average age of the whole number was 72 years and five months; there was one at 90, and 15 of 80 years and more. The oldest man in this district I have heard of was Joseph Melhuish, of Pitcombe, who died on 23rd February, 1838, at the age of 108.

The shoe shop of brothers Ted and William Pitman, at No. 1 High Street, and Buxton Brothers jewellers at No. 3, in 1955.

William Pitman (left), Marion Matthews of Overton Terrace, and Ted Pitman outside their shop in No. 1 High Street in 1930.

❖ SHOPS & TRADES ❖

Above: *The summit of Bayford Hill in about 1905, eastwards from Queen Victoria's golden jubilee seat and the Highlands* (left), *to the Firs* (centre) *and Haycroft, with Bayford House opposite* (right).

Left: *Ireson Villas, built in 1874 on the east side of Ireson Lane* (left) *and Coylton Terrace* (right), *with the former partially creeper-clad in about 1890 before the immediate view was largely blocked by trees.*

The south side of Bayford Hill in the 1930s, westwards from Hill Crest (left) *before the demolition of the Prince of Wales tavern* (centre) *for road widening, with a Bullnose Morris parked below the Highlands* (right).

Above: *Up Church Street from the Temperance Hotel* (left) *and Sansom's Ironmongers and an 'Antiques' sign at Prior's House* (right) *as two-way traffic clogs the pinch point below the Market Place in 1960.*

Left: *Victorian lady passing Thanksgiving Cottage and No. 14* (second left) *as a cart and cyclists pose between the Temperance Coffee House* (centre) *and Matthew William Pickford's drapery store at Nos 11 and 13 Church Street, in a view eastwards in 1900.*

Standard and Crane's fireworks with squibs and other pyrotechnics on offer in the street outside Scammell's hardware store, next to the Furniture Mart in Prior's House at No. 7, on the tercentenary of the Gunpowder Plot in 1904.

Chapter Six
Around Wincanton

Church tower view, looking down to Nos 30 and 29 Church Street and upwards to Lambrook House and the Masonic Hall (right centre), *both half hidden behind trees in 1904.*

Lambrook House (left), *which lost its outside glass dome through storm damage in the 1950s, looking upwards to thatched Wyvern* (centre) *and the Temperance Coffee House and Hotel* (right) *in about 1905.*

Above: *Boy cyclist and ladies outside Pickford Drapery Men's Ware (left), looking westwards in the 1950s to Thanksgiving Cottage and Wyvern (centre), with the Temperance Hotel (right) still in being in name at least.*

Right: *Church Street upwards from the churchyard gates, signed for the town centre, in 2005.*

Below: *Looking down Church Street in about 1900 to St Peter and St Paul's parish church (left) and creeper-clad Lambrook House and Wyvern (right) as a policeman passes a funeral carriage, and mourners enter the churchyard.*

◈ AROUND WINCANTON ◈

Above: Edwardian cyclists halfway up Church Street, outside the premises of draper Matthew William Pickford.

Left: Potomac News (centre) *reaching Wincanton in 2001 at Thanksgiving Cottage in Church Street.*

Sight and Sound and a Therapy Clinic in the former Temperance Hotel (centre), followed by Miah's Tandoori, on the north side of Church Street in 2000.

Above: Churchyard view of No. 32 Church Street with the postbox and litter bin and Nos 30 and 29 (centre) looking uphill from the churchyard in 2000.

Right: Yard view of No. 7 Church Street (left), glimpsing beneath the roof to Little Wymering, across the road at No. 6 which was the Victorian home of Samuel Hooper.

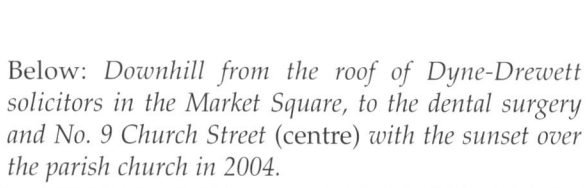

Below: Downhill from the roof of Dyne-Drewett solicitors in the Market Square, to the dental surgery and No. 9 Church Street (centre) with the sunset over the parish church in 2004.

AROUND WINCANTON

Dormer windows at No. 3 (centre foreground), *the Millers Inn and Richmond Place, and Town Mills* (centre right) *in a glimpse around Silver Street to the Union Workhouse* (upper left) *beyond the railway line, seen from the church tower in about 1922.*

Nos 8 and 6 Silver Street (left), *the Rope Walk and James Stores* (centre) *in about 1900, looking south to the parish church and the corner beside Richmond Place* (right).

Above: *The junction of South Street, looking north from hairdresser Roy Sansom and Bertha White milliners in Albion House (centre right) to Smith's Library in the Market Place, in the late 1950s after the rebuilding of the bombed offices of solicitors Dyne, Hughes and Archer in Sutor House (right).*

Right: *The Dogs (left) and Plaza Cinema, on the east side of Tout Hill, in 1998.*

Old St Audrey's (left) on Tout Hill, and the offices of Rutter and Rutter solicitors in St Audrey's (right), from the south-east in 1998.

The Nog Inn (formerly the New Inn) showing its outsized Dutch-style roof soffets, seen from the south-east in 2000 with the Lotus Chinese restaurant next door.

Above: *South Hill House as a thatched former farmhouse, seen shortly before demolition in 1890, and the home of tailor John Grinter in No. 23 (left) which was demolished in 1922 to provide an access road into Balsam Fields.*

Right: *Rear view of South Hill House, in the 1880s, with a then-fashionable monkey-puzzle tree on the lawn.*

Below: *The entrance to Balsam Fields (left) and Nos 1 and 2 South Hill Villas with a shield and 1891 date-stone on the bay window with the initials 'W.H.B' for William Herridge Bracher.*

Above: *Hats and caps worn by all the workers building the Elementary School on the west side of the Tything in South Street, in 1896.*

Right: *South Road Villas (far left), Granny Jacob's Cottage (centre left) and the Elementary School on the west side of the Tything, in 1910.*

Below: *The home of chimney-sweep Alfred Jordan – initially in the Tything and then in Church Street – boasted a royal warrant in the 1890s.*

Road sign for 'A 371 Castle Cary' and Granny Jacob's Cottage (right), in the 1950s, before clearance for parking spaces.

AROUND WINCANTON

Right: *Mill Street from the Trooper Club (left) and bay windows of Nos 7 and 9, with the cart opposite outside No. 10, in a view westwards over Town Mills in the 1890s.*

The George Inn, at the bottom of Mill Street, with landlord William Rex and family in 1889.

Mill Street from Scammell's furniture store at No. 28 (left), and old cottages opposite, eastwards to the Market Place and the Town Hall in 1895.

Above: *The Baptist Church in Mill Street, built in 1832, with schoolrooms (right) which were added in 1897.*

Right: *Gravestone at the Baptist Church commemorating its founding pastor, George Day, who died in 1858.*

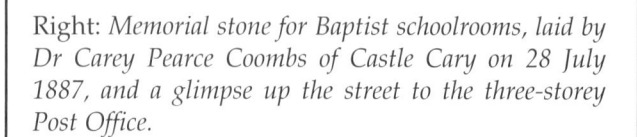

Right: *Memorial stone for Baptist schoolrooms, laid by Dr Carey Pearce Coombs of Castle Cary on 28 July 1887, and a glimpse up the street to the three-storey Post Office.*

Below: *Hamstone roundel for 1887 – the year of Queen Victoria's golden jubilee – set in the wall of the Baptist schoolrooms in Mill Street.*

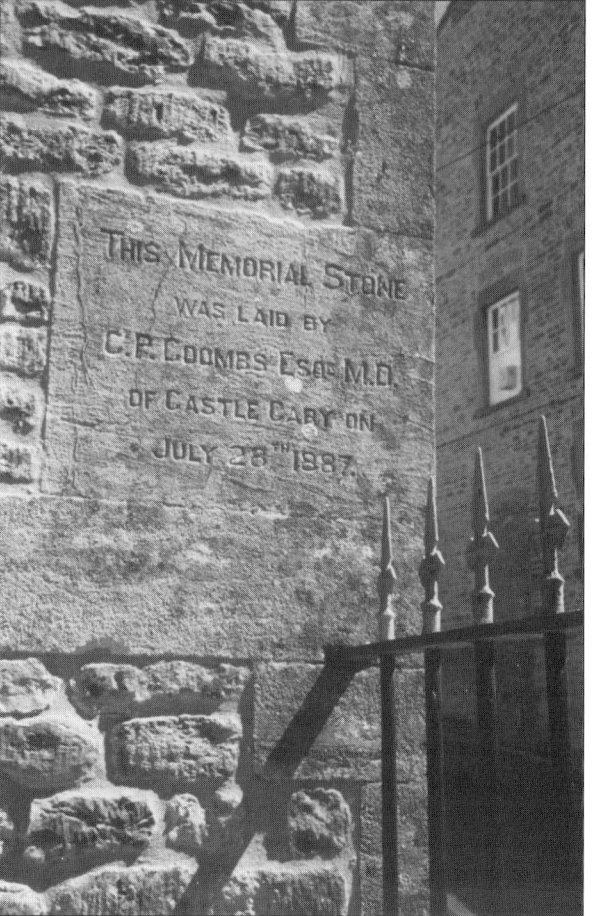

AROUND WINCANTON

Top: *A £1 note No. G176 of the virtually insolvent Wincanton Bank issued on 25 July 1809.*

Above: *Wincanton & Somerset Bank note No. U2827 issued in December 1824.*

Left: *Banking by card in the new millennium with money being withdrawn from a hole in the wall at the National Westminster Bank in South Street.*

Above: *Wincanton Brewery, looking westwards from Greyhound Mews, to a view of the valley with a primitive-looking engine puffing along the Somerset and Dorset Railway.*

Right: *Dereliction in the old brewery yard, after closure of Edward Sweet's auction room, in 1982.*

Below: *The National School wall (left) and former brewery buildings, in use as Edward Sweet's auction rooms, in 1980.*

AROUND WINCANTON

Above: *Mrs Gwen Taylor with daughter June and Granny Lewis at the door of their greengrocery store at No. 2 North Street, on the site of Ralston Court, in 1939.*

Right: *Jewell's House and Britannia House* (left), *with Northbrook Villas and Hillside Villas next up the hill and Northbrook House* (right) *in 1999.*

North Street from the railway embankment above Hiscock's Cottages (left) *and the Police Station, c.1900, southwards to St Joseph's, Rockhill House, Northbrook House and Wincanton Brewery* (top right).

Above: *Hiscock's Cottages* (left) *and the 1856-built County Police Station* (centre), *northwards to the Court House* (right) *and the gable end of No. 19 North Street.*

Below left: *Arthur Tucker's son Geoff* (right) *holding a high-rise Raleigh, on loan for Wincanton Carnival in about 1912, outside their cycle depot on the south side of Hiscock's Cottages.*

Below right: *Water pouring from Shatterwell Shoots* (centre) *in Shadwell Lane in 1904.*

Bottom right: *Hiscock's Cottages, renovated in 1986 and now known as Shatterwell Cottages, from the south-west in 1999.*

AROUND WINCANTON

Right: *Rodber House, from the south-east, in 2001.*

Right: *Dial House and Batch Cottages, in c.1905, looking eastwards to the railway bridge and Silver Street with Town Mills visible through the arch.*

Below: *View from the railway bridge of the entrance to Rodber House (bottom right), Batch House and Dial House, and Nos 1 to 3 Batch Cottages and Batch Cottage (centre left), c.1900.*

Above: *General view of the Batch in about 1905, east to the railway bridge with the gable ends of Dial House* (left) *and Nos 1 to 3 Batch Cottages* (opposite), *with Batch Cottage further up the hill* (right).

Top right: *Wisteria trailing across the frontage of Batch House in 2000.*

Above: *Summertime view of Dial House* (left) *and Batch House, combining to present bright frontages in 1998.*

Above right: *The sundial that gives Dial House its name, dating from 1691, out of commission on a dull day.*

The northern arm of Rickhayes, westwards from the tower of the parish church in about 1930 – before the estate spread across the adjoining field – with the railway line to the east (foreground).

Houses in Rickhayes fronting West Hill, in 1935, uphill from Batch Cottages and Batch Cottage (left) *to Dawn and No. 10 West Hill* (centre), *with Densan above.*

Above: *West Hill before widening, looking downhill in about 1910, with the houses being Cader Eden* (centre left), *West Holme, Julian Villa, Pouncett House, and a gas lamp beside the entrance to the Mount.*

Below: *Pre-development view of Springfield Road south-east to the Batch* (centre left) *and Rickhayes* (centre right), *with the railway line crossing the middle distance, in 1966.*

AROUND WINCANTON

Friends of Verrington Hospital holding a fête in its field, in an aerial view northwards from above Cale Way, c.1990.

Town View, as Wincanton Union Workhouse was known in its latter days, looking westwards across its allotments from the railway embankment above Shadwell Lane, c.1900.

THE BOOK OF WINCANTON

History uncovered, revealing the 1884-dated Milk Depot façade, in 1985.

Above: *Tono Chocolate and other Cow & Gate products being packed in the 1950s.*

Left: *The last load of aluminium milk churns being backed into the unloading bay at the Unigate factory on 31 July 1979.*

Cow & Gate's factory and chimney in the 1950s, looking south-westwards from above the town's gas holders, across Station Road with allotments and petrol pumps, to the goods yard and railway towards Templecombe (top).

AROUND WINCANTON

Off-loading the churns, on to a conveyor belt production line, at 'The End' (chalked on the platform) in July 1979.

Churns begin their transit from outside to inside at the Unigate milk factory.

THE BOOK OF WINCANTON

The Dairy Princess from the Mid-West Show poses with the very last milk churn to be processed by Unigate at Wincanton in July 1979.

Milk from the churns passes into pasteurising vats.

Demolition of the factory chimney, reaching the top of a faintly visible letter 'C' (beginning Cow & Gate) in 1986.

Chapter Seven
Wartime Wincanton

The twentieth century opened with the South African War, against Boer rebels, and the Wincanton Hunt Steeplechase of Easter Monday in 1900 captured the national mood. Punters attending the event, at Hatherleigh, raised £105 for the *Daily Telegraph* war fund.

A public meeting in Wincanton on 19 December 1900 passed the following resolution which was proposed by surgeon Charles Wright Edwards and seconded by the rector, Revd Walter Farrar (1865–1916): 'That a hospital be founded for the service of Wincanton and the surrounding neighbourhood.'

The Cottage Hospital was established in No. 18 High Street, and comprised two wards, each with three beds. For many years it faced an uphill struggle for funds and was repeatedly under threat of closure. The town's other medical institution, the Isolation and Fever Hospital on the hilltop at Verrington, was a sanatorium for tuberculosis sufferers. Four patients died there in one outbreak.

In the town, Revd Joseph Beaupre arrived at the Baptist Church in June 1901, and the New Market Company held its first cattle market in the Tything, on 2 October 1901. The Provincial Grand Lodge was hosted in Wincanton for the first time, in 1902, under the presidency of Lord Dungarvan.

Out of town, in February 1901, the 340-acre Holbrook estate was purchased by John Angerstein, a descendant of the Russian-born Lloyd's underwriter John Julius Angerstein (1735–1823). The family's founder is remembered for launching a £2,000 fund to reward the invention of the lifeboat, and for what happened after his death, to the bulk of his exceptionally important art collection. A total of 38 Old Master paintings were bought by Lord Liverpool's Government, for £60,000, and formed the nucleus of the National Gallery in 1824.

The late John Julius also seems to have contributed a macabre memento to the Holbrook collection of keepsakes. It was the custom at that time for plaster casts to be taken of freshly deceased eminent and interesting persons – the latter category including those who had been hanged – and a plaster face was found beneath the office floor at Holbrook House in the 1960s. Yellowed patches of crazed patina indicate an early-nineteenth-century date and John Julius Angerstein would be the obvious candidate.

The John Angerstein who came to Holbrook set about dealing with a poaching problem. Poster-sized notices were issued in December 1903, offering a ten shilling reward, for information that could lead to the conviction of those 'using wires for catching rabbits at Holbrook'. Angerstein put his efforts into its last major enlargement and rebuilding, completed in 1904, adopting a style that is late Victorian rather than that of the Edwardian reign which had started. His architect was Sir Reginald Blomfield (1856–1942) who was particularly fond of working on English country houses that were surrounded by impressive grounds. He was constantly distracted by the possibilities for garden design and firmly believed that a house was only as good as its setting.

He formalised the south front of Holbrook House, by raising the nearest lawn, terracing it above the tennis-court, and burying the outer wall of the basement so that the height of the house was reduced to what he considered to be the right proportion to its width. A Tudor stone-mullioned window, cut at Ham Hill, that had provided token light for the basement was filled with Edwardian mortar and was henceforth 6 feet underground. Similarly useless are the great doors at the south-west corner of what are now the cellars; these merely open into a shoot beside the hardcore of the present main car park. They were originally the side doors into the under-region of the house but changes to the south front, which had until this time been the side with the driveway and entrance hall,

'This window commemorates the men of Wincanton who were numbered among those who at the call of King and Country left all that was dear to them, endured hardness, faced danger and finally passed out of the sight of men by the path of duty and self-sacrifice, giving up their own lives that others might live in freedom.'

Mobilisation with the Royal Field Artillery marching to war, via Wincanton Station, in August 1914.

Wincanton Fire Brigade, outside Tout Hill House – now the Catholic School of Our Lady of Mount Carmel – with its 12-man crew in about 1905.

Pit-stop at the Greyhound Hotel (left), during military manoeuvres in the summer of 1910, with the field gun having been clamped with brake and shoe and elevated to displace the weight.

Gunners heading for an exercise on Salisbury Plain in 1910, just four years from a war in which artillery will cause most of the deaths, preparing to stop outside the Greyhound Hotel and the shop front of stationer George Sweetman.

The generation that went to war in 1914, fielding the 'Single' team (against 'Married' opponents) beside the Cricket Pavilion at Old Hill on 27 May 1911.

meant that they had to be covered to avoid unduly cluttering the revamped reception zone.

Blomfield used levels and terraces to advantage in his gardening but he felt that a formal house should rise from a flat platform, even if doing so left the 200-year-old cedar of Lebanon emerging from the lawn at a point 8 feet up its trunk. It still thrives, now more than 300 years old, and is hurricane proof as a result of the support around the base. The expanse of the house ruled out the narrow south face continuing as a practical access to the whole building in the future. Blomfield's solution was to move the entrances to the middle of the far longer west side and to shun the alternative of fragmenting the grounds by providing front and back driveways. Opposite the new west porch, to give it apparent justification, Blomfield created steps at the top of which he placed a formally mounted wrought-iron gate, flanked by golden yews. They lead nowhere. Only the old orchard lay at the top of the rise.

It was Blomfield's ethos that the garden had to be seen to matter and he was at the time the leading expert on his subject. He had written *The Formal Garden in England*, in 1892, *A History of Renaissance Architecture in England*, in 1897, and other reference works.

Although Sir Reginald is the architect who has been credited with Holbrook's present shape the matter is subject to an element of doubt. His son, Austin Blomfield, wrote in 1946 that the work was probably done by his great uncle, Sir Arthur Blomfield, who he said had died in 1908. This statement is not, however, without its problems as Sir Arthur, the architect for the Bank of England, in fact died in 1899 and therefore could not have rebuilt Holbrook. Work in progress was taken on by his two sons, Charles Blomfield (died 1932) and Arthur Conran Blomfield (died 1935) but their firms are no longer in existence.

For John Angerstein, however, it was Gertrude Jekyll who provided inspiration in the garden and his library contained copies of her books on *Wood and Gardens, Wall and Water Gardens,* and *Gardens for Small Country Houses.*

The Holbrook library featured aspects of the family history, with the *Annals of Lloyd's Register,* a number of maps of Russia, and an almost endless supply of the *Catalogue of Angerstein's Gallery of Paintings.* Several copies were auctioned in July 1945, when the contents of the house were dispersed, but 20 packets of engravings failed to find a buyer and were left in the building. They had been with the actual 22 copper-plate blocks from which the prints were taken off. Geoffrey Taylor, who later found that he had bought them with the house, was told the old engravings were worthless and proceeded to tear them in half for use as menus and for taking copies of letters. This was perhaps a sacrilege but not a frugality – paper was a scarce commodity in postwar Britain.

Until that sale in mid-1945, spread over six days in the first summer of peace in Europe, the house exuded elegance with a plethora of inlaid mahogany, down to the butler's tray and stand. Paintings were everywhere, mostly being copies of the family treasures that

WARTIME WINCANTON

Until the First World War, the Wincanton Cork Club – based at the George Inn – was an informal friendly society which collected cash by imposing fines for bizarre 'offences' such as failure to carry a cork.

'We don't want to lose you, but we know you have to go.' Laughter as a lady says her goodbyes to a gunner, with onlookers using wagons owned by coal merchant John Snow as observation platforms at Wincanton Station yard, in August 1914.

had been sold to the nation, hanging from the heavy brass rails that still run beneath the high ceilings of just about all the downstairs rooms. The front hall had marble busts of Fox and Pitt as reminders of an age when politicians could become statesmen. Just as obvious were the cluttered assortment of stuffed birds, animal heads and horns. The principal hunting trophy was the stuffed otter, in its own large case, from one of the Stour's upper tributaries.

The Edwardian hothouses in the old walled garden were for vines. By 1945 two white and one black variety had entwined to fill its south-facing glass. By this time the house was being emptied of its contents. It already had a new owner. Cooper and Tanner Ltd auctioned the house and its estate, split into ten lots, at the Working Men's Club in Wincanton on 11 July 1945. The owner of Holbrook House became Frome butcher Freddie Somerset.

Revd John Roskruge Wood, the son of the one-time British School master in Mill Street, was elected president of the Baptist Union of England and Wales in 1902. Having moved on from City Road Baptist Church, in 1874, he had been minister of one of London's biggest Baptist assemblies, in Upper Holloway. Notable members of the Deanesly clan – which began with a union of the Deane and Sly families – included Samuel Deanesly, and son Edward who was a surgeon in Wolverhampton, and daughter Margaret. The latter, as Professor Margaret Deanesly (1885–1977), became the leading expert on the pre-Conquest and medieval Church in England.

The foundation-stone for the 70-feet high double towers of the Catholic Church of St Luke and St Teresa, on the side of Acorn House in South Street, was laid by Bishop Ambrose Burton on 7 November 1907. Inside, the nave is 46 feet long and 20 feet wide with a ceiling height of 54.5 feet. It is of Early English design with six arcades in Bath stone on octagonal shafts that support the roof. Apart from ashlar dressings, from Bath, the general walling stone is Forest Marble from local quarries at North Cheriton and Maperton. The architects were Canon Scoles and Geoffrey Raymond and the builder Charles Bryer from Bridgwater.

Percy Lamb designed the high altar, reredos and a hanging rood-screen, which were installed shortly before the consecration service in 1913. He also designed the Holy Infancy altar and arranged for the Austrian firms of Ferdinand Demetz and Stuflesser to carve the pulpit, stations of the cross, and Lady altar. Percy Lamb's brother, Father Francis Lamb, was the Prior at Wincanton during the building of the church. The old chapel became St Luke's Hall.

One of the first cars to be seen regularly in Wincanton was an imported automobile by Hotchkiss of Paris. It carried the registration Y674, an early Somerset number, and appears in a photograph from about 1910, parked outside Stuckey's Bank in South Street. Chauffeur John Easterbrook sat at the wheel while manager F. Thirwell Fowler attended to the account of Arthur Sutton from Shanks at Cucklington. Fowler was also the treasurer of Wincanton Union Workhouse, Wincanton Rural District Council and Wincanton Hospital. He was an insurance agent and mortgage broker, for Somerset Permanent Benefit Building Society, and treasurer of Wincanton Coal and Gas Company.

It is a photograph that is engraved on my mind. It was given to me by Arnhem veteran Barry Cousens. Each time it has appeared in print over the past three decades it has been jinxed by errors. Opposite is the New Inn (not yet renamed the Nog) where Mrs Mary Brooks was the landlady. The main scope for confusion has been the motor car and its owner. Having sorted out the problem, and warned Barry Cousens not to succumb to local folklore, he was intercepted by historian Puffy Bowden who assured him the driver was Captain Richard Chichester. The proofs were changed and that was how the caption read.

Usually one hears no more of such things when the subjects are safely dead. In this case, however, descendants and friends of both families tried to set the record straight by writing and telephoning. They told us that Captain Chichester was 15 years old in 1910. His parents were Charles and Mary Chichester of Horsington.

In fact the car was then owned by Sir Arthur Sutton (1857–1948), 7th baronet as he became, with the death of his nephew in 1918. That has also caused some genealogical mix up as the title regressed a generation. The 6th baronet was Captain Sir Richard Sutton (1891–1918) of the 1st Life Guards who owned 'about 13,000 acres, exclusive of London estates'. As well as Shanks, he had another country seat at Benham-Valence, near Newbury, and a London home in South Audley Street. The 8th baronet, Sir Robert Lexington Sutton (1897–1981) also lived near Wincanton, at Clinger Farm. The 9th baronet, Sir Richard Sutton (born 1937), lives at Langham, Gillingham.

'Scandalous behaviour' in nearby Holton entertained Wincanton with what came to be known as 'the battle of the churchyard'. Retired wheelwright John Norris took on Holton's rector, Revd Joseph Sorrell, in a series of physical, vocal and written skirmishes throughout 1912 and into the following spring. Years before, back in 1899, the late Mrs Norris had been buried in Holton's overcrowded churchyard. John Norris had assumed that he would eventually be reunited with her in the adjoining plot. Instead, in January 1912, a hole appeared at the very spot and John Norris realised that a Mr Raymond was about to join his wife.

Although John Norris had moved to the next parish, to Maperton, he returned every day to Holton to make his protests. He collared the rector, apparently literally outside the Old Inn, and also threatened to disrupt the funeral. A police constable was called to attend the ceremony and his presence beside the grave prevented any disorder. John Norris refused to accept defeat and embarked on a sustained campaign which saw Joseph Sorrell put into a state of siege as he ran the gauntlet of Holton Street between the Rectory and St Nicholas's Church.

Mr Norris had lost the day but went on to win the war. Against resistance from the rector and almost united and universal superstitious objections from other villagers – who considered it ungodly or at least unlucky to disturb the dead – he applied for diocesan approval to move Mrs Norris from Holton churchyard. Another obstacle came from concerns of 'a danger to public health'.

John Norris was given permission to take his wife's body to a much roomier cemetery, under beech trees on a hillside, a mile away at Maperton. In April 1913 the deed was done – at nine o'clock on a bright spring morning, Mrs Norris made her move. The local sanitary inspector, Ernest Harvey Knapman of Bayford Hill, stood by as an observer. Although it was removed from waterlogged ground the coffin was still intact and sealed.

Even the closure of the dispute was accompanied about a legal row. This centred on jurisdiction. In the Town Hall at Wincanton, rural district councillors argued that they should have been consulted. The Home Office also considered that its approval was needed for a body to be exhumed. The diocesan clerk stood his ground and insisted that a bishop's faculty was sufficient bureaucratic authorisation for a closed coffin to be moved from one area of consecrated ground to another inside the ecclesiastical see of Bath and Wells.

The Priory in South Street became a Red Cross Hospital. One of its priests was killed while serving as a chaplain, in Flanders, and Father Laurence Lamb sailed to the Middle East. They were remembered during the unveiling of a stained-glass window in the Lady Chapel of the Catholic Church:

This window, dedicated to St George and St Martin in 1919, is the gift of the Wincanton District of the British Red Cross Society, to commemorate the loan of the Monastery buildings as a hospital during the Great War, 1914–18. 898 sick and wounded of the British Imperial Forces were nursed here.

Princess Alice, Countess of Athlone, was the special guest at a Red Cross gift sale in Wincanton in June 1917. It raised much of the £1,100 surplus which the local Red Cross Hospital fund held at the end of the First World War. Mrs Ridley of Maperton House ensured that it was used as an endowment for the town's Cottage Hospital. Pine House, a three-storey building, was purchased to replace the premises at No. 18 High Street. It was opened by Lady Theodora Guest of Inwood, Henstridge, as the Wincanton and East Somerset Memorial Hospital, on 8 February 1922. A total of 80 in-patients were treated during its first year.

The Racecourse at Hatherleigh was revived after the First World War, with Reginald Hutchings as the secretary of Wincanton Race Company, operating from an office in Church Street. Hugh Grosvenor, 2nd Baron Stalbridge (1880–1949), from Motcombe House, thought they could find a better venue. Late of the 14th Hussars, being mentioned twice in despatches during the Boer War, he cajoled fellow directors into buying Kingwell Farm on top of Old Hill. The traditional Easter Monday meeting moved there to herald a new era in 1927.

The Boy Scout movement inspired an equivalent structure for young girls with the 1st Wincanton Brownies being formed in November 1925 and registered as a pack on 12 January 1926.

Ernest Dyke, Sir Robert Sanders MP, Sir Arthur Sutton, and the Duke of Somerset hosted a dinner in the Town Hall 'for South African farmers visiting the West of England' on 15 July 1927. They saw a town and countryside that was firmly rooted in agriculture:

The population amounts to about 2,000 and the principal industry is the production of powdered milk, the manufacture of which employs some 200 men and women. The farms in the Wincanton area are principally dairy and the manufacture of the renowned Somersetshire Cheddar cheese is centred here. This cheese in competition with the whole world carries off the majority of the principal championship awards. Another important agricultural industry for which Somerset is famed is the cultivation of apple orchards and the manufacture of cider.

Wincanton-produced powdered milk, carrying the emblem of 'Smiler', was set to become the nation's favourite diet for babies. 'Dairy weaning foods' followed after the Second World War as this advertisement proclaimed:

If you cannot feed baby yourself you can safely place your trust in Cow & Gate, and when baby is ready for weaning, see that he graduates to solids on Cow & Gate Cereal Foods. Now! Cow & Gate dairy weaning foods in the six delicious varieties mothers have asked for. Creamed Ground Rice, Semolina, Sago, Tapioca, Barley Milk Puddings, and Egg Custard. So smooth in texture and so pleasant in flavour they provide an excellent introduction to solids for the tiny baby and the perfect sweet for the toddler and older child. Ready cooked – can be served hot or cold. From all chemists – 6 ounce tins for only 9d.

The town's tallest landmark, from its erection through to lowering and then brick-by-brick demolition more than half a century later, was the chimney that dominated the milk factory and creamery. Its original height, 150 feet, was reduced to 132 feet, a few years before its removal. Erection in 1928, on the sprawling site between Station Road and the railway embankment, was followed by two significant events. Firstly the young man who had been the principal steeplejack fell to his death on the next job. Secondly the West Surrey Central Dairy Company, which had become Wincanton's main employer, transformed itself into Cow & Gate Limited in 1929. The Cow & Gate siding from Wincanton Station was laid in 1933.

The company also based its tankers and transport operations in the town. A subsidiary, Wincanton Transport and Engineering Company Limited, had been established in 1925 and the garage section was given its own separate identity, as Wincanton Garages Limited, in 1946. 'The Big Cow' was the first Wincanton tanker to carry a name, 'perhaps with some malice'.

Sir Robert Sanders, 1st Baron Bayford of Stoke Trister (1867–1940), was elevated to the House of Lords in 1929. The Unionist MP for the Wells division, since 1924, he was chairman of Somerset County Council and a former Under-Secretary for War, after which he was Minister of Agriculture and Fisheries. He lived at Bayford Lodge and was long remembered in the town for the egg-throwing incident which left him splattered when he addressed an election crowd outside the Town Hall. The precision shot hit him as he spoke from the first-floor window of the Greyhound Hotel. It was credited to Gladys Bessie Rumbold, who was marched off to the Police Station in North Street, but later released without charge. She had not actually thrown the egg, son William said, although he added that he wished she had.

By 1928, Wincanton Memorial Hospital had outgrown its second home in Pine House, and was coping with twice its original throughput of patients. Major operations, once a rarity, were now being carried out regularly. It was decided that it was imperative – despite the dire economics of the times – to provide the town with a new purpose-built hospital.

The foundation-stone of East Somerset Memorial Hospital, in Balsam Park, was laid by the Marquess of Bath on 15 October 1931. The architect was A.J.B. Abbott. Completed over the winter, the building was opened with a silver key by HRH Princess Alice, Countess of Athlone, on Saturday 16 July 1932. The building had 12 ground-floor beds and two private wards, to cater for a total of 152 in-patients and a similar number of out-patients during its first year.

Baker John Hartnell came to Day's Bakery in South Street from Montacute, in 1931, with son Fred and daughter May. The family kept the business going for six decades with Fred at the back and May Hartnell behind the counter to the end, still serving loyal customers 'who have been coming in for as long as we can remember'. They eventually retired in 1988.

The straight length of modern carriageway in the cutting that carries the A371 main road from Holbrook to Lattiford was gouged out by huge machines in 1975 as a by-product of the bigger scheme to re-route the A303 through the fields to the south of Wincanton. Such a spur road was, however, a serious proposal in 1932 when Somerset County Council decided as the first priority in its list of new roads 'to construct the Holbrook House – Lattiford road with a carriageway 20 feet in width'.

By January 1932 everything seemed to be going ahead for what would have been the first length of new-style 'arterial road' in the district. The council had resolved:

> ... to complete the acquisition of the lands required from Mrs Angerstein for the construction of the new road from Holbrook House to Lattiford, to instruct the County Surveyor to make provision in the estimates for the financial year 1932–33 for the construction of the necessary kerbed footpath in front of Holbrook House, to pay all legal charges and expenses and land agents' charges incurred in connection with the matter, and to seal, and authorise the Clerk to sign, any necessary documents.

The project had such a high priority that compulsory purchase powers were approved. Mrs Angerstein raised no objection but H. Perry of Hook Farm and G. Barnes of Hatherleigh Farm opposed the scheme as did Wincanton butcher Jack Bartlett, who was the owner of Lattiford Farm. They wore down the council's resolve and the half mile of road remained unbuilt for another half century. North–south traffic continued to branch off via Jack White's Gibbet and Holton village, and the turnpike road which skirted Holbrook from West Hill was little more than a country lane which carried only the local traffic between Wincanton and Castle Cary.

'Meet My Sister' was the first film at the new Plaza Cinema, immediately uphill from the Dogs in South Street, when it opened on 22 November 1934. Tickets ranged from ninepence to two shillings and the manager was Stanley Coates. On the screen, it was the year of Gracie Fields ('Sing As We Go'), as Britain's highest-paid star, with film debuts for George Formby ('Boots, Boots') and Will Hay ('Those Were the Days' followed by 'Boys Will Be Boys'). Stanley Coates was an accomplished performer in his own right, having been half of a skating duo, and proved the point by skating on the roof of a moving car as it moved up the High Street, in order to promote a movie.

Yeoman of Signals William Harry Atkins, on HMS *Glowworm*, was killed in one of the classic acts of naval heroism during of the Second World War. The destroyer happened to be off the North Cape, in support of a mine-laying operation, as the German navy moved into position for the invasion of Norway which was scheduled to begin the following day. *Glowworm* found herself facing the heavy cruiser *Admiral Hipper*, with destroyer escorts, west of Trondheim. Completely out-gunned, she rammed the

WARTIME WINCANTON

The rear of the Westminster Bank, south-eastwards to the Carmelite Priory (centre right) *after being devastated by a German bomb on 15 May 1944.*

Westwards across the street to the International Stores (background) *from the bombed remains of the Westminster Bank – where the manager's daughter was killed – and No. 3 South Street.*

Closure notice for the Whit Monday bank holiday (in window) *came into effect a fortnight early with the direct hit on the Westminster Bank in 1944.*

Fund-raising badge for Wincanton War Weapons week, in 1941, featuring the new Churchill tank.

Warship week had a particular poignancy for Wincanton which was the home-town for a disproportionate number of naval ratings.

Hipper in a suicidal manoeuvre, which resulted in the British ship sinking at 09.05 hours on 8 April 1940.

William Atkins, the 32-year-old son of Harry and Rose Atkins, was the husband of Edith Emily Atkins of Wincanton.

Major Leonard Buckley of the Royal Army Medical Corps was killed on 13 October 1940, by a German bomb at Stanmore, Middlesex. The 54-year-old doctor lived at Ash House in the High Street and is buried at Wincanton cemetery. His wife Suzanne, was mortally wounded in the same incident and died on 7 November 1940.

The 24-year-old Pilot Officer Roland Niall Chancellor from Wincanton was among the eight-man crew of Stirling bomber W7428. Flying with No. 15 Squadron of 3 Group, Bomber Command – from RAF Wyton, Huntingdonshire – the dark shape that was LS-Z took off at 09.50 hours on 18 December 1941. They were tasked for a daylight raid against German warships at Brest. All eight were killed after being engaged and surrounded by Messerchmitt Bf.109 fighters. Their Stirling was last seen dropping towards the sea with its port wing burning furiously.

Although provided with fighter escorts by the RAF, the bombers had met strong resistance from the Luftwaffe, and a total of four Stirlings and a Manchester were lost during the operation. Roland Chancellor, whose name appears on the Runnymede Memorial for flyers with no known grave, was the son of Eva Linton Chancellor and Herbert St Vincent Chancellor. The parents lived in Sherborne.

Leading Seaman Victor Harold Francis Crocker went down with the destroyer HMS *Jaguar* when she was torpedoed in the Mediterranean, off Sidi Barrani, at 04.45 hours on 26 March 1942. The sinking was carried out by the German submarine U-652. The 21-year-old was the son of Ellen and Harold Crocker of Wincanton.

During Warship Week, in 1942, Wincanton Rural District Council adopted HMS *Fowey*. The 1,105-ton sloop dated from 1930 and was on convoy escort duties. A bronze bell was presented to mark the link and a reciprocal shield given to the town by the Lord Commissioners of the Admiralty.

Both the Somerset and Dorset Railway and the line from Castle Cary to Weymouth attracted bombers, sometimes in their own right but usually as clearly visible navigation aids which pointed southwards towards the English Channel and the safety of Luftwaffe airfields in France. Engine driver Walter John Shergold (46), from Sherborne Road, Yeovil, was killed by a bomb at Castle Cary Station at 09.30 hours on the third anniversary of the outbreak of war, 3 September 1942.

Then Templecombe was hit at 21.20 hours on 5 September 1942. Nine were killed that evening. They were Mrs Elizabeth Coombs (55) of School Lane; James Dart (48) and Samuel Day (49) of Westcombe; Arthur Dray (36) of South View; Mrs Millicent Greenslade (36) of South View; Mrs Eva Howe (58) of West Park Cottages; Mrs Florence Howe (34) and Michael Howe (5) of School Lane; and Mrs Annie Rowerfell (66) of Church Hill.

The first warship of the Royal Canadian Navy to be sunk by aircraft, and also the first lost in the Mediterranean, was the corvette HMCS *Louisburg* which was torpedoed by the Luftwaffe at 19.25 hours on 6 February 1943. She sank 60 miles north-east of Oran. Among the dead was 20-year-old Able Seaman Thomas William Sheppard from Wincanton. Corporal Arthur Sydney Atkins of the 1st Battalion, East Surrey Regiment, was killed in North Africa on 26 February 1943. The 29-year-old, who came from Wincanton, is buried in Massicault War Cemetery, Tunisia.

WARTIME WINCANTON

Above: *The ruins of the Westminster Bank, after being hit by a German bomb, looking southwards to the twin towers of the Catholic Church* (top left).

Left: *Bomb damage from the rear of the Westminster Bank, looking westwards from White Horse Yard, to the chimney of the International Stores* (top right).

Below: *A total of 18 men and women from Wincanton, who lost their lives in the Second World War, are commemorated in the parish church.*

Joe Louis, the World Heavyweight Boxing Champion, refereed a series of military matches at Wincanton Racecourse, on 29 April 1944, and stayed the night at the Greyhound Hotel. In a series of five bouts the United States Third Armored Division took on the Fourth Armored Division.

Louis was born Joseph Louis Barrow, in Lafayette, Alabama, in 1914. Since turning professional, in 1934, he had fought 57 professional contests by the time he came to Britain, and lost only one of them (when he was knocked out in the twelfth round by Max Schmeling in New York on 19 June 1936). Louis held his world title for a record 11 years eight months seven days from 22 June 1937 – when he knocked out James J. Braddock – until announcing his retirement on 1 March 1949. He made a total of 25 successful defences.

Air Training Corps cadet Eric Poole from Lower Shepton Montague obtained Joe Louis's autograph on the only piece of paper he had to hand. This was his gliding and flying log for ATC Squadron No. 1808. It also records two 'fairly good' solo glides, 35 minutes in a Miles Master, and 55 minutes in a Bristol Blenheim, in 1943.

Across the globe, in bitter hand-to-hand fighting for the bungalow and tennis-court of a remote hill station in Nagaland, Private Anthony Owen Fraser, was killed at Kohima on 2 May 1944. He was serving with the 2nd Battalion, the Dorsetshire Regiment, which successfully held back the far point of the Japanese advance into India. The 25-year-old, who was living in Wincanton, was the son of Ethel and John Osborne Fraser of Horsell, near Woking. He is buried in Kohima War Cemetery.

Wartime Wincanton had its stray bombs with the most damaging falling at 01.55 hours on Monday 15 May 1944. Two exploded harmlessly but the third caused the complete destruction of the offices of solicitors Dyne, Hughes and Archer at No. 3 South Street. It also badly damaged the adjoining Westminster Bank. There the manager's daughter, 29-year-old Daphne Grace Spencer, was killed instantly as she slept and thrown 100 yards by the blast. Her body was found at dawn, at 05.45 hours, on land to the rear of the White Horse Hotel.

The explosion woke 10-year-old Roderick Matthews in 24 Mill Street. The next thing he heard was his mother, as she asked 'Are the stairs gone?' The house was undamaged but the experience has lived with Rod Matthews for the rest of his life. He can still recall the moment, when he was dreaming about a warship which he had been drawing that evening, and imagined its guns firing as he heard the bombs exploding. A Mosquito night fighter from RAF Zeals was already on the tail of the German bomber which was shot down at Templecombe.

The symbolic loss was a cross from the top of the Carmelite Priory in South Street. Picking up the pieces of the story in the morning, Special Constable C.L. Rutter – who had been on duty at the time in the Market Place – established that there had been three bombs. The first fell in Spring Close, the second in South Street, and the third at Brains Farm. The latter did not explode for another 15 or 20 minutes.

A temporary Police Station and rest centre was established in the Bear Hotel. The A303 traffic, which normally ran in both directions along South Street, had to be diverted via Church Street and Station Road. The United States Army provided the manpower and vehicles for clearing South Street. What caused most consternation, for those living and hiding secret lives, was that letters from burst files at the solicitors' offices had become public property. They were literally blowing in the wind:

Apart from the one very regrateable fatal casualty, the most troublesome and possible serious consequence of the raid was the fact that a very large number of confidential and valuable documents were blown all over the town.

Private William Ernest Atkins of 2nd Battalion, Wiltshire Regiment, was killed following the invasion of Italy, on 27 May 1944. The 28-year-old son of Wincanton's Annie and Ernest Atkins, he is buried in the Beachhead War Cemetery at Anzio.

Aircraft losses around the town included a flak-damaged four-engined Flying Fortress bomber of the 8th United States Army Air Force. This comprised the 8th Bomber Command, 8th Fighter Command, and 8th Air Service Command. Their daylight attacks on Germany were conducted from further east – across the North Sea – principally from airfields in East Anglia.

The Flying Fortress which came to grief at Wincanton was a camouflaged B-17G airframe belonging to the 401st Bombardment Squadron of the 91st Bombardment Group. Each such Bombardment Group consisted of 72 aircraft and 2,700 personnel. The Wincanton link is with Flying Fortress serial number 42-37958. Given the name 'Old Faithful', she was on her 37th operational mission since joining the squadron from America on 16 December 1943.

Twelve such Flying Fortresses of the 401st Bombardment Squadron lifted off from their English base at Bassingbourn, Cambridge, which had been transferred by the Royal Air Force to American control in 1942. The target for their daylight raid on Sunday 25 June 1944 was a Luftwaffe airfield at Blagnac, near Toulouse, in Vichy France. There the German flak immobilised number three engine, next to the fuselage, on the starboard wing.

The pilot, Second Lieutenant Peter Mikonis of Margate City, New Jersey, initially considered taking the crippled aircraft to neutral Spain. After further discussion, with co-pilot Second Lieutenant Frank E. Pepper junr of Berkeley, California, and the navigator, Second Lieutenant Joseph E. Sullivan, he decided to try to make it home. Although at a greatly reduced height they managed most of the 900 miles, in a curve

Above left: Victor Crocker, from Wincanton, on being posted to the battleship HMS Rodney *in 1939.*

Above: The last photograph of Victor Crocker who lost his life when the destroyer HMS Jaguar *was torpedoed in the Mediterranean on 26 March 1942.*

Left: Wincanton war veterans Paddy Smyth (left), holder of the Military Medal (who landed the first tank on Sword Beach on D-Day), and Percy Jee, beside memorabilia from both world wars, in 2005.

Below: An artist's impression of HMS Glowworm, *destroyer H92, with Harry Atkins as Yeoman of Signals, ramming the German heavy cruiser* Hipper *in an act of suicidal bravery off the North Cape in 1940.*

north-westwards and then north-east – over the Bay of Biscay and then up the English Channel – to within sight of safety.

Having crossed Lyme Bay and the Dorset Downs they headed for the grass runways of wartime RAF Zeals at 550 feet altitude on the greensand plateau above Stourhead Gardens on the Wiltshire–Somerset border. To reach it they had to rise from the Blackmore Vale. In sight of Zeals, less than 5 miles away, their luck ran out. The damaged starboard wing, which had been trailing black smoke since before reaching the English coast, finally collapsed over Common Lane in the pastures below Wincanton town. 'Old Faithful' turned over and crashed in a field between Snag Farm and Physicwell House. She exploded into a fireball at the moment of impact.

Michael Watts, the eldest of Austin Watts's boys, told me he was playing in the fields at Snag Farm that evening when his sister heard and then saw the bomber coming towards them at hedge height from the west:

She screamed and we looked around. There was an almighty crash as it exploded in our yard which became a big ball of fire. An engine landed only yards away from our farmhouse, it was that close, and the blast took down a wall and burnt out a store. Trees were blackened and leaves singed in the orchard. There was debris everywhere. It put the milking bail out of action for months.

He was 11 years old. Ken Bennett, a year older, was working in an adjoining field:

I was 200 yards away. We heard this roar and looked back and saw this big black thing. There was a huge bang and then it was like it was snowing with white stuff everywhere. I think that they had a lot of injured on board and that was why they did not bale out before the plane blew up.

Bob Chamberlain, aged ten, was attending Sunday school at the time. The whole town heard the explosion and he joined the first group of onlookers and potential rescuers to run towards the sound of gunfire: 'We went down to the crash site within about ten minutes of it happening. There were shells going off and body parts all over the place.'

All nine crew were killed instantly. Three have been mentioned. The others were Second Lieutenant Will H. Stevens (bombardier) of Smithfield, North Carolina; Staff Sergeant Roy C. Anderson (top turret gunner and engineer) of Sacramento, California; Staff Sergeant Douglas R. Deurmyer (radio operator) of Topeka, Kansas; Sergeant Ralph Stein (ball turret gunner) of Savannah, Georgia; Sergeant Richard A. Mehlberg (waist turret gunner) of Milwaukee, Wisconsin; and Sergeant Dean A. McDowell (tail gunner) of Omaha, Nebraska.

Sergeant Joe Harlick, from Hot Springs, Montana, was one of the photographers for the 91st Bombardment Group. Two photographers were assigned to record the damage to the aircraft, details of body parts and damage to buildings for compensation purposes. Joe, who was aged 23 at the time, recalled the visit on his return to England in 2004:

We had a Jeep and driver. We came down to Wincanton from Bassingbourn on the 26th, the day after the mission, but there were no road signs anywhere in the country, and I didn't remember where it was. All I remember is that it was an all-day assignment. You naturally walk around to see what you are to photograph to begin with. There was a lot of damage, aircraft parts, and smaller body parts including a parachute with a piece of a skull with hair on it. The larger parts had already been recovered by the undertaker I guess.

The two of us shot numerous pictures, some 20 to 40, which were sent to London. During the printing process I kept four shots from Snag Farm. I had a personal camera as well as the government's five-by-four plate camera. Not that I knew more about this Flying Fortress than 958; not even LL-G for her squadron code and call-sign. In our formations we always identified aircraft from the last three numbers of their serial numbers. No names were used in our records.

We lost 2,012 men who never came back to the base. Upwards of 800 were killed. So I made a point not to get acquainted with crew members. In 1943 for a plane to make 12 missions, successfully, would be stupendous. By mid-1944 that had risen to 25 – as a result of better fighter protection and armament – but as far as Old Faithful was concerned to reach 37 missions was well into borrowed time.

There were more military around at Snag Farm than spectators. I've shots of other unidentified crash scenes. Distance wise the Wincanton site was one of the furthest assignments from base. On Christmas Eve in 1944, during the Battle of the Bulge, we were all fogged-in and the aircraft went to an RAF base, so we looked forward to a Christmas party without our planes.

It was my first champagne, and I was serving the drink, but at one o'clock in the morning we were alerted to go to the planes in a convoy through the middle of the night. English bombs were not compatible with ours so we had to take the weaponry.

We were lost with a little slit of headlights and freezing windscreen, stopping to knock on doors to find where the hell we had to go. We took turns to get out and urinate on the windscreen to try and keep it clear. We were negotiating down little English roads when a 500-pound bomb fell out in front and stopped our Jeep. It was my lucky nickel! We rolled it off into the ditch and left it there. By the time we arrived the crews were sleeping in their planes and we then heard that the mission was cancelled.

The nine crewmen of 'Old Faithful' have their local memorial on a plaque set in the roadside wall of the

WARTIME WINCANTON

The central outbuildings at Snag Farm, photographed from the farmhouse for the United States Army Air Force by Joe Harlick on 26 June 1944.

The yard and south-western milking parlour at Snag Farm on 26 June 1944, strewn with debris and remains of the crippled American B-17 bomber which crashed there the previous evening.

Final photograph of 'Old Faithful', trailing smoke from number three engine, after being hit by flak over Toulouse.

Highlands, on Bayford Hill, overlooking the crash site half a mile away on the other side of the dual carriageway. When this was unveiled on 4 July 1954, the tenth anniversary of the crash, it was recalled that Wincanton people were grateful to the pilot for having avoided hitting the town. Sadly, he never had that option, having lost sufficient height and momentum to clear the ridge, and those at the front of 'Old Faithful' must have realised that their only hope lay a hilltop away.

Corporal Raymond Speed Andrews of the 2nd Battalion, Argyll and Sutherland Highlanders, was killed on 18 September 1944. The 24-year-old son of Annie and James Speed of Wincanton, he left a widow in the town, Theresa Hannah Andrews. Raymond Andrews is buried in Kasterlee War Cemetery, Belgium.

Our last living link with wartime bombardment, living at May Cottage, North Street, until retirement to Taunton in 2004, was Squadron Leader Brian Redmond. He flew Blenheims and then Lancaster bombers, at night, with 101 Squadron and 550 Squadron, for the duration of the war. It was against the odds to survive many missions, let alone the entirety of the conflict. The statistics show a 50 per cent fatality rate; of the 110,000 combat crew who served in Bomber Command, 55,573 were killed. Brian Redmond had the honour of marching in Whitehall on Remembrance Sundays during the 1990s to salute their memory and place the Bomber Command wreath on the Cenotaph for the service that was denied its combat medal.

The war at sea claimed the life of Petty Officer Basil Hedley Martin, a submariner aboard HMS *Porpoise*, on 14 January 1945. He was the son of John Hedley Martin, and wife Kathleen, from Wincanton.

A rare illness and a chance encounter in 1946 led Geoffrey Taylor (1908–94) down the Great West Road and into the country for something completely different from his occupation of the war years. He was the head buyer for Firestone Tyre and Rubber Company Limited, which quite apart from tyres had helped the war effort with rubber gun fittings and other specialist products, from one of the biggest factories in west London. Wartime nights were then spent as head Air Raid Precautions warden at Iver, Buckinghamshire. This combination of daytime paperwork and constant night duty triggered a deterioration in his vision. In 1986, Geoffrey Taylor looked back for me to the chain of events in the spring of 1946 that brought him to Wincanton, as the new owner of Holbrook and its grounds which had shrunk to 15 acres of parkland. He proceeded to turn the buildings into Holbrook House Hotel in the most challenging of times:

> *I appeared before a conference of European eye specialists with a label round my neck. Finally I was told that I had to give up paperwork and get out to the country. All that we knew of the country from a business viewpoint was entertaining. We had no knowledge of farming or anything like that. So hotels were the obvious choice.*
>
> *We toured all over the place, then one day the head man at Usher's told me I was quite ridiculous, being just another crazy amateur who thought he could run an hotel. I then had lunch with a chap at the Old George in Frome. It's since been pulled down.*
>
> *He mentioned Freddie Somerset, a London evacuee butcher, who had bought Holbrook a year before. He thought he would turn it into an hotel and country club and was in cahoots with the publican of the Master Robert, a famous roadhouse on the Great West Road. They'd got cold feet and put it back on the market. I had coffee with Freddie in Frome and came down to Holbrook.*
>
> *It was bare and empty but it had six lovely mahogany doors. I fell in love with those doors. The house had its own acetylene gasworks and a private water-supply which came from the other side of Higher Holbrook, via a 25,000 gallon reservoir belonging to the house, piped down by gravity. In the severe winter of 1946–47 we would have troubles with it freezing up but that's another story.*
>
> *I paid a bit over the odds for Holbrook, £7,500. I could have got it for less. We concluded that in about July 1946 and my first wife, Jimmie – she was a James – moved in during September to look after the horses. My eyes were already clearing up, helped by forcing myself to do as much far-focusing as possible, and everything was happening here. Firestone gave me leave of absence to come down as much as necessary.*
>
> *We inherited Albie Jones. He had come to the Angersteins as a boy to wash down their vehicles. By then he was getting on in years, a typical hobbling gnarled countryman, who had been caretaking while this place was empty. He still stoked the boilers, at the bottom of a vertical ladder, 12 feet below the ground.*
>
> *In under three months the whole shooting match was open. You couldn't do it at that speed nowadays. We opened officially with the Wincanton Silver Band on Christmas Eve, 1946, and they have returned each year since. It became a Holbrook tradition. On New Year's Eve we opened to the public – about ten of them – with a dance. We had about 30 residents that Christmas. Most of them were friends who came down from London.*
>
> *In Wincanton we found ourselves being stopped in the street and greeted by traders. 'We hope we'll do business with you, Mr Taylor,' was the gist of the message. Fortunately the local Food Officer was very helpful. There were thousands of these tiny rationing coupons. It got tighter after the war. One day an inspector called and saw our trays and trays of eggs. 'Of course, we keep our own chicken,' we explained. Luckily he didn't ask to see them, the five scrawny specimens in the yard. Our Irish porter kept a pig and a local farmer cultivated mortality-weakness among his calves, disposing of the carcasses to Holbrook. We had to help him out.*
>
> *Liquor was scarce. Whisky was just not available but I got a hogshead – 43 dozen bottles – from a distillery in Scotland for £1,000 which was quite a price but it drew people like flies around a honeypot. To bolster up and*

Looking westwards towards the damaged yard and house at Snag Farm (centre) *from the direction of Coneygore Hill on 26 June 1944.*

Firemen and foam, among the remains of the B-17 bomber 'Old Faithful' which crashed at Snag Farm, on 25 June 1944.

Above: *Sandra Goddard (left) and Mike Watts, with Air Force veteran Joe Harlick (right), comparing his contemporary photographs with the scene at Snag Farm in 2004.*

Right: *Mike Watts (left), who lived at Snag Farm in 1944, shows Joe Harlick unrepaired damage in 2004.*

Below: *'Health and history' walkers at Bayford Hill in 2005, having crossed the road from the memorial to 'Old Faithful' below Highlands (top right), look south towards the crash site.*

equip the bar the liqueurs had to come from the Soho Wine Stores and it sticks in my craw that a half-bottle of Creme de Menthe was £7.10s.0d. You wouldn't want to pay that now. We had to sell at cost, just to dress the shelves.

Geoffrey Taylor drew on contemporary files, ledgers, letters and visitors' books. These confirmed the draconian nature of austerity restrictions, such as the licence (Supplementary, 0/7/32514/1) under the Defence (General) Regulations, 1939. Issued on 23 December 1946, this permitted 'installation of 23 basins in bedrooms... at a total cost not exceeding £361.0s.0d'. This was conditional:

1a. *Basins already held by applicant.*
b. *Contractors will not ask for or employ local labour.*
c. *No lead will be used.*
d. *No priority asked for any fittings or materials.*
2. *Subject to agreement on controlled materials.*

Everything was rationed or regulated, including the price of meals, and a variety of ingenious evasive measures had to be brought into play:

The regulation was that no hotel or restaurant could charge more than five shillings for a main meal. Established places like the Ritz could apply for a cover charge, graded according to their status, but we had no track record and had to stick to the five shillings. It was impossible for a place starting up to get a liquor licence, going back to the restrictions of the Defence of the Realm Act of 1916, but you could get a club licence. Correctly that meant sign a form and wait 48 hours before you could get a drink. One took chances if people came to stay overnight but you had to watch it. Losing our club licence wouldn't have been funny at all. We had to get by on a club licence for six years, before applying for our full licence. By then, in 1953, we were established and it went through as sweet as nuts.

There were other ways around restrictions. The cashier at a certain bank collected foreign stamps and had a side-line dealing in spirits from pubs around that didn't use up their quotas which had been set at pre-war levels. He'd phone up and ask if we had received any interesting foreign stamps. When we called at the bank he'd say that, 'by the way a friend called in and left this parcel for you to collect'. It would contain an odd collection of half-empty bottles. They came in handy but, by God, they cost a lot of money.

The Blackmore Vale Hunt Ball of 28 November 1947 was held at the new Holbrook House Hotel. The food bill for 206 people was £108.0s.0d. They more than matched that at the bar with £110.7s.8d. for beer and liqueurs plus £34.17s.6d. for nine bottles of Scotch that were consumed that evening. Claret, for comparison, was represented on the first Holbrook wine list by 1943-bottled Chateau Gruaud-Larose and 1945 bottles of Chateau Talbot at £1.6s.0d. each.

Forster Altenburg hock from 1945 was £1.7s.6d. The 50-year-old Denis Mounie cognac was the top-price brandy at 4s.6d. a glass. Liqueurs were 2s.6d. a glass.

The shoemakers C. and J. Clark Limited of Street came to Holbrook House Hotel for their 125th birthday celebrations in 1950, attended by advertising agent Cecil Notley and architect Donald Hamilton as special overnight guests who were booked into 'nice single rooms'. The company also treated Harold Power from London tanners Bevington Sons Limited, which had supplied them for a century, along with competitor Harry Holder who had done the same through John S. Deed and Son (Tanners) Limited.

Big events caused logistical nightmares for a new postwar hotel. Lacking many quite basic fittings, which had not been manufactured since 1939, these had to be brought in for special occasions. Glasses, bowls, cutlery and '3 dozen brass ash-trays' were delivered by van by John Haskins from Town Street, Shepton Mallet. In November 1947 he had to express regret that the tea urn was already hired out. Earlier that year, when H.E. Dyke from New Barn Farm, Wincanton, booked Holbrook on 7 February, it was on the understanding that he was to supply:

1 pin of cider;
Cigarettes;
6 chicken ready for cooking;
1 tongue;
Requirements of fruit salad;
Trifle;
Cake and milk (we to ice the cake);
You also to supply card tables and cards if required.

Sometimes, however, the hotel was asked to provide more elaborate diversions. 'It is now quite definite that the Raw Materials Committee will be invading Holbrook House,' Geoffrey Taylor was told on 1 September 1948, in a message that asked him to arrange for 'a comic game of bowls somewhere if you could suggest a nearby rink'. More ordinary in-house entertainment for such events cost the equivalent of three bottles of Scotch ('a fee of ten guineas'). This was the standard rate for 'professional musicians from Bristol'. They were augmented by the Fred Symonds' Trio, Jock Lawson's Band and the Streamliners Dance Orchestra from Castle Cary.

By this time the business was diversifying into equestrian sidelines, on some scale, as Geoffrey Taylor was paying £135.16s.11d. per quarter for hay and straw for the horses. Once again he had the invoice to prove it, from Henry Willis and Son of Westbury in Sherborne, plus some rather acrimonious correspondence about the quality of the fodder:

Lots of it was sub-standard and we were always having to send bales back for credit and refund. My daughters were in their point-to-point phase and had their photograph on the front page of the Horse and

Hound. *I remember that the fair price for a second-hand pony saddle was £7.10s.0d.*

In 1947 we had been joined by Mrs Stead, a war widow, who was later made a director of the company running the hotel. We started off with horses, for livery and riding instruction, and for a time Captain H. Brown ran a Holbrook Equitation School. Two interesting characters were Pam Childe, who took over the horses for a time, and Major Tony Simmons who joined us and made his home above the horses' quarters. Even after we'd relinquished the horses he stayed for some years, helping with bar-tending and as our handyman. He was a wonderful old character.

My two daughters, Shirley (who now calls herself Clare) and Judy, were fetched out of a boarding-school at Ramsgate, and went to the Hall School, Bratton Seymour. At Iver we had been just down the road from Coppins, the home of the Kent family, and had shared their governess. Lady Herbert or Princess Marina said they would like Alexandra and Edward to join my girls for a holiday in the country.

On 9 April 1947 they arrived with Madame A. Bascourt de Saint Quentin, their lady in charge, and stayed for three weeks. Princess Marina was here at the start and finish. Because it was a royal party the Chief Constable of Somerset had to be involved, and put in a police telephone that was manned all night. For this locality it was a big thing and put us on the map. Sleepy old Wincanton had woken up to us.

Prince Edward, the present Duke of Kent (born 1935) and a cousin of Queen Elizabeth II, returned to Ludgrove School at Wokingham, from where he wrote the following letter to Geoffrey Taylor on 18 May 1947:

Dear Mr Taylor, How are you? I am having a lovely time at school and swimming began today. This week we have been playing cricket. Next Monday I am going to Queen Mary's birthday lunch in London as a great treat. We are at present in quarantine for German measles.

Please could you send me the water-pistol I had when I came to stay with you, because I left it behind. My bedroom was number 8 and the pistol was black and looked like this [drawing]. *Please give my kind regards to Judy and Shirley.*

With love from Edward.

With the creation of the National Health Service, in 1948, Verrington became a 32-bed geriatric hospital.

Some 60 years later, commemorating the air crash of 25 June 1944, the yard at Snag Farm had its busiest day for years.

Chapter Eight
Transport

Above: An Edwardian carter – identified as John Hatchard's wagon from Walford Mill, Wimborne.

Left: Butcher working for Johnny Bartlett, in White Horse Yard, about to go out with deliveries, c.1914.

Below: Somerset County Council highways department steam wagon at Town Mills in the 1920s.

Steam road-roller carrying the name-plate of 'John F. Burch, Bradford, Taunton', with Wincanton driver Harry Eddington at the wheel in the 1920s.

Tommy Jordan (left) with the grain wagon carrying the name 'Town Mills, Wincanton' in the yard off Silver Street in about 1905.

TRANSPORT

Above left: *Wincanton Station offering 'Trains for planes' and a £1.19s.0d. day-return ticket to London, in 1965, from a series of shots by Len Taylor.*

Above: *Wincanton Station and a gentleman with luggage (left) waiting for a porter as the train from Bath heads south in 1925 towards Templecombe and Bournemouth.*

Left: *Next stop Cole, for veteran 44557, which was the first Midland Class standard 4F 0-6-0 engine to reach the line from makers Armstrong of Newcastle in 1920. The view is southwards, from an empty down platform at Wincanton, as she heads a local train in 1961.*

The lines through Wincanton Station, looking southwards on the approach from Cole.

British Railways Class 4 4-6-0 locomotive 76019, Swindon-built in 1955, heading a passenger train for Bath. It is climbing north-westwards up the bank above Cutts Close, Verrington Lane, in 1962.

Staff at Wincanton marking the retirement of the stationmaster, Charles Christopher Lethbridge (centre) in 1951. The picture includes: Happy Hamlin, Norman Ralison, Jock Bains, Wyn Padfield, Norman Ashfield, Harry Light and Norman Gould.

British Railways Class 4 2-6-0 locomotive 76019, Horwich-built in 1953, steaming beneath the footbridge at Wincanton Station, with a passenger train destined for Bath in 1963.

Double bridges over the River Cale and Silver Street, at the Batch (left) in a view eastwards from Hook Field to the embankment north of Wincanton Station in 1912.

✧ TRANSPORT ✧

Right: *Redevelopment of the former station yard, with Pines Close* (left) *and Cavalier Way* (centre), *beside the Railway Inn* (right) *in 1990.*

Left: *Peter Rochford's Garden Machinery business, built across the site of the town's gas holders, as it looked in the 1990s before moving to Wincanton Business Park.*

Below: *Station Road* (right foreground), *from the air in 1955, when it was an industrial zone with the railway* (bottom left) *as important as the road.*

THE BOOK OF WINCANTON

Above: *Literally the last train on the line, as diesel engine D6320 removed the track through Wincanton, in July 1967.*

Right: *Parking charges at Wincanton Station, posted beside the buffers in the goods yard, with 1965 prices starting at two shillings for cars.*

Below right: *Cast-iron listing for the directorate of Wincanton Coal Gas Company Limited, in the time of chairman Thomas Green, when it was re-equipped from Sheffield.*

Below: *A collectors' item, still in situ in Wincanton two decades after the line had closed, recording its final days as an offshoot of the Southern Railway.*

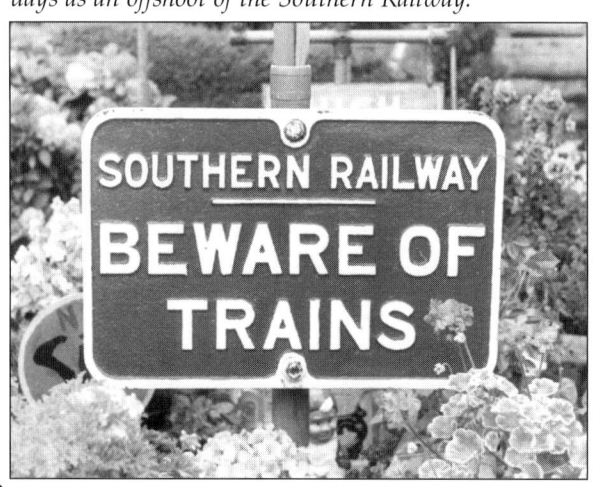

TRANSPORT

Above: 'Move on to next pump if vacant' a sign reads, but only a tractor could pass along the road beside Anchor Hill Service Station in May 1979.

Left: Esso pumps at Anchor Hill Service Station 'Under New Management' – that of Daphne Chivers – beside what was then the A303 in 1956.

Cars for sale, covered by water, behind Anchor Hill Service Station in 1979.

Anchor Hill Service Station, beside the stream from Holbrook to Lattiford, was inundated by a flash flood in May 1979.

Above: *Claben Limited decorating the Christmas tree in the Market Place in December 1988.*

Right: *Container lorries are the normal traffic of the district but Claben Limited's refrigerated container took a turn too far.*

Above: *Hooks Haulage caught on camera at the pinch-point beside the Town Hall.*

Right: *Hunt's Dairies taking the corner in a view from South Street to Smith's Library (left) in the Market Place.*

✦ TRANSPORT ✦

Above: Bailey Bridge over the River Cale at Hawker's Bridge (centre left) *and the Tanker Depot from the north-west in 1973.*

Left: Access road into Bennett's Field (left foreground) *and the Tanker Depot* (centre) *from the west, in 1978, after completion of the new A303 but before construction of roundabouts.*

Below: Dairy Crest tanker units (left) *and a Wincanton Logistics lorry* (right) *in the roadside sheds of Wincanton plc, in 2002.*

129

Above: *The town's main car park, established beside what was the first Safeway supermarket, opposite the Health Centre* (right) *in Carrington Way in 1990.*

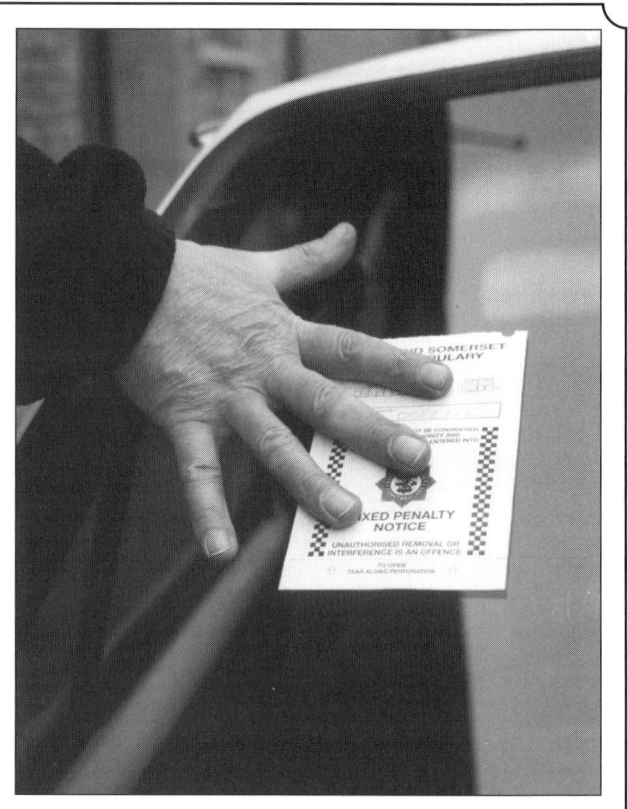

Right: *'Fixed Penalty Notice' for exceeding the half-hour parking limit in North Street.*

Crunch time for a First Direct bus and a Volvo, in Church Street, in 2003.

TRANSPORT

A night-time blaze at Oasis Takeaway and Kebabs in No. 6 High Street (right) *brought the town to a standstill in 1998.*

Appliances attending the takeaway fire included a cantilever gantry which provided an adjustable platform both for fire-fighting and clearing debris in the aftermath.

Debris blocking the High Street after the kebab-shop fire in 1998.

The White Horse Hotel (right) saved from the blaze (left) in 1998.

Firemen in South Street, clearing up after a blaze in flats behind the National Westminster Bank, in 2001.

Chapter Nine
Modern Wincanton

The New Inn in South Street, dating from 1793, came of age in 1949 and changed its name to the Nog Inn. North Street was still a secondary trading street, with greengrocer and florists O. and R.J. Wedderburn at No. 2, facing D. Butler's fish and chip shop. The Surplus Stores did brisk business in the Market Place. S.R. and J. Culpin provided breakfast, lunches and teas seven days a week, from the Canton Café in the High Street.

The second Elizabethan age, as it was proclaimed with the coronation of Queen Elizabeth II in 1953, was marked by the biggest series of public events in Wincanton since the celebration of Queen Victoria's two jubilees. Sunday 31 May 1953 was 'Coronation Sunday' with a special order of service issued by the Queen. A public holiday followed on the Tuesday, with the festivities beginning with a salute of 21 maroons fired by members of the British Legion. Wincanton Silver Band led the children into the recreation-ground for a fancy-dress parade. A gymnastic display was provided by senior pupils from Wincanton County School. There was also a display by Wincanton Fire Brigade to a backdrop of side-shows and amusements.

Tea and ice-cream for the children was followed by a film show in the Cow & Gate factory. There were also 'teas for the older residents in the Town Tent (by invitation)'. Community singing in the evening was led by members of the Wincanton Girls' Choir with the Wincanton Silver Band. The dancing stopped at 9p.m. as tannoys relayed a broadcast of the Queen's coronation speech. It was a 'token' fireworks display, at ten o'clock, that rounded off the outdoor celebrations. One of the ironies of recovering from recent total war was that peacetime pyrotechnics were in short supply.

Meanwhile, the coronation ball was taking place in the Deanesly Hall to the Commodore Dance Band at 5 shillings a head ('fancy dress optional').

Progress and redevelopment were the theme of the decade and although Wincanton suffered much less than many towns it saw a spate of demolitions. A curving terrace of 18 cottages at Whitehall, between Shatterwell House and Old Hill, were replaced by Whitehall Garage and two bungalows. The Rectory, between Clementina's hardware store and what was then the Midland Bank, was also removed. This left a noticeable gap in the High Street frontages which has remained empty to this day.

The last master of the former Union Workhouse, a Mr Maunder, took it into Sir William Beveridge's welfare state framework. He died in 1957 and the sheltered housing in Maunder's Close was named in memory of the last couple who managed the institution as master and matron. It evolved into Town View Infirmary which closed in 1973 and was then demolished.

Postwar education arrived with the opening of King Arthur's Secondary Modern School on 22 April 1958. It changed to comprehensive status in 1979, after population movements to south Somerset swelled its roll to 720 pupils, and now styles itself as King Arthur's Community School. Edgar Murray was the first headmaster, when Field-Marshal Lord Harding of Nether Compton – retired Chief of the Imperial General Staff – performed the opening ceremony. On retirement, Mr Murray continued to look after the welfare of former pupils, by running the Citizens' Advice Bureau in Mill Street.

The Memorial Hall, the good cause of postwar carnivals, was opened on 9 January 1959. To a full house, it hosted a drama festival in February 1962, with a triple bill of one-act plays. The Wincanton Players presented 'Rock Bottom' by Dorset author Nina Warner Hooke. It was a satire based on amateur dramatics set in her own home village of Langton Matravers in the Isle of Purbeck. Geoffrey Taylor, the owner of Holbrook House Hotel, was the producer. Eileen Olive starred as eccentric authoress Augusta Wilmot who was loosely based on Monica Hutchings. The male roles were taken by John Day as the professor, Monty Carswell as the *Western Gazette* reporter, and Tom Rutter as George Purvis.

Jean White, as Miss Fisher, supported Eileen Olive's character. Judy Dyke, as Mildred Purvis, carried off the difficult task of hovering between teetotal and quite sloshed. 'It was not overdone,' said the adjudicator, Cecil Bellamy, although he felt that Ann Banks 'as a temperamental Brampton thespian, could have shown a little more agitation'. Kathy Rhodes was Miss Price and the stage manager was Dennis Gilbert.

Horsington Women's Institute and Mere Drama Group provided the accompanying productions. Wincanton Players were commended by the judge and went forward to the next round in the county competition. The same group of stalwart participants and supporters produced one or two plays a year for the next couple of decades.

Merchant Navy class locomotive 'Clan Line' (number 35028), pulled out of Bournemouth West Station on 6 March 1966. Johnnie Walker, a driver since 1938, was at the controls as it headed for Bath with the last passenger train to travel the Somerset and Dorset Railway. Wreaths and a ceremonial coffin were paraded en route, as afternoon turned to

Terrace of houses, No. 13 to 17 Malthouse Close built in 1984 and fronting North Street, with the only surviving Victorian brewery building being that with the flat-roof behind its maltster's house (top right).

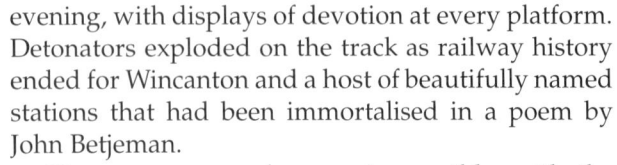

Flats at Malthouse Close (centre), *built in 1983, and an almost fully developed skyline on West Hill, in 1990.*

evening, with displays of devotion at every platform. Detonators exploded on the track as railway history ended for Wincanton and a host of beautifully named stations that had been immortalised in a poem by John Betjeman.

The process soon became irreversible, with the lifting of the track in 1967, although some bridges and viaducts have survived. Steam trains were also on the way to the scrapyard. One of the name-plates from the West Country class locomotive 'Wincanton' (number 34108), was given to the town and now has pride of place above the bar in the Town Hall.

The 13-feet-3-inch clearance, as proclaimed by red warning signs on either side of the railway bridge in Southgate Road, failed to put off a succession of larger users of the A303 from attempting to squeeze through regardless. By the time of its demolition, in March 1969, it was literally notched by close encounters. These included lorries, double-decker buses and a Churchill tank. Circus giraffes, on the other hand, passed through this eye of a needle almost uneventfully. Their heads were too high but decapitation was narrowly averted. The crate shuddered to a halt and the animals were led through on foot.

The Unigate bulk milk reloading station was opened in November 1970 after the merger of Cow & Gate with United Dairies as Unigate Foods Limited.

The Health Centre and Library in Carrington Way were built in 1972. Princess Margaret opened the latter on 27 June 1973. That year the new Police Station also opened at the end of the new road.

Town Mills, at the junction of Mill Street and Silver Street, was demolished in 1973 and became a builders' merchant's yard. On the other side of the disused railway embankment the Union Workhouse also closed in 1973 and was demolished. In latter years it had been Town View Infirmary but local people still talked of the stigma of 'ending our days in the Workhouse'. Its site was earmarked for the Maunders Close section of a new housing estate which continued to climb West Hill for the rest of the century.

Flood water, in March 1973, caused the collapse of historic Hawker's Bridge over the River Cale between Bennett's Mead and Aldermeads at Southgate. What was described by the county historian as 'a very good bridge of two stone arches' in 1792 had last been rebuilt by Richard Stone, from Yarcombe in Devon, in 1833. A temporary steel bridge was installed to keep the A303 traffic flowing, and this was then replaced by a military Bailey Bridge – also restricted to single-file working – until it was replaced by a permanent concrete-slab bridge in 1979. By then the A303 had been moved out of town, in March 1977, on to the Wincanton bypass.

A new central block and additional block at Verrington Hospital were opened by Lord Aberdare, the Minister of State at the Department of Health and Social Security, in 1973.

Following Britain's entry into the European Community, Wincanton was twinned with the French towns of Gennes and Les Rosiers, in 1975.

After managing Holbrook House Hotel for 17 years, David and Diana Smith moved to Bath to run their own restaurant, and were replaced by Philip Jackson from North Cadbury and Geoffrey Taylor's second wife. Geoffrey married Joan Wingham (1942–2001) after the death of his first wife in 1970. 'Dressed to the nines,' in her own words, Joan Taylor became Holbrook's flamboyant presence for the rest of the century. She achieved a formidable reputation for delivering cutting one-liners. These were enriched by a past which included laboratory work on Nobel-prize winning genetics in Boston and an earlier marriage, which ended in divorce, after seeing her delivering a memorable performance as a Colonel's wife in the British Army of the Rhine.

Decades later, after suffering a stroke which left her disabled, she briefly considered the option of going into Dunkirk House and phoned the Royal British Legion to ask if the military marriage had lasted long enough to qualify for placement. 'One week is the minimum requirement,' she was told. 'That was quite long enough!' Mrs Taylor retorted.

Holbrook became the annual base for a succession of groups from Holland who returned each spring to

The entrance to the Police Station.

Wessex Wyvern and lamp, 1856 date, and the County Police motto.

explore the internationally famous Wessex gardens of the National Trust and private stately homes. There were also literary gatherings such as dinners of the Parson Woodforde Society, celebrating the eighteenth-century Castle Cary clergyman who was renowned for a gourmet diary and weather gleanings, rather than his sermons. On 8 July 1995, Holbrook House Hotel had the distinction of being the first venue in Somerset to be granted a marriage licence, enabling it to hold civil wedding ceremonies.

As successive lengths of dual carriageway upgraded the A303 trunk road into its present status of the preferred route from London to the West Country, and the strategic location of the town led Roger Cuss, the Station Officer for Wincanton Fire Brigade, to establish his own vehicle recovery operation. Cuss Car Care, which soon moved into purpose-built workshops on Wincanton Business Park, was founded by fireman Roger Cuss in 1979 with the motto 'You bend 'em, we mend 'em'.

Most of the buildings of former Wincanton Brewery were levelled in 1983. These included the sale rooms of auctioneers Scammell and Sweet where the last gavel had been wielded by Edward Sweet. Those roadside buildings have been replaced by a terrace of modern town houses, with a car park covering the main site of the brewery and its chimney, plus a block of flats built on allotments below, in what is now Malthouse Close. The development was carried out by Sturminster Newton builder John Ashford.

Wincanton Rugby Club was formed in 1983. Miniaturist and watercolour and oil painter Norah Ruthven (1903–90) lived in Wincanton from 1946 and was among the founders of Bruton Art Society. Steven Knight, an old boy of King Arthur's School, won the 1987 Grand National on 'Maori Venture'.

The most famous visitor to Wincanton in recent times has been 'Desert Orchid'. Born at Goadby, Leicestershire, on 11 April 1979, 'the Grey Horse' was initially named 'Fred' by groom Ruth Jackson. 'Des', as he became, was unplaced at Wincanton in 1983 but returned as a winner on 23 February 1984. There were many more successful returns, ending with a first on 8 February 1990 and coming second on 24 October 1991, followed by a retirement visit to bask in glory. In all he had been placed in 53 of his 70 races with 34 of those having been firsts.

Although non-racing persons at the other end of the telephone still ask 'Where?' at the mention of Wincanton, it is no fault of the company whose vehicles carry the town's name. Put bumper to bumper, I once calculated, the tankers and other lorries would stretch halfway to London. Sometimes it seems they are trying to do just that, but fortunately they are spread around the country, operating from numerous depots. There are also thousands of cars and vans rented across the land. The company started as a subsidiary of the old milk factory, eventually being part of Unigate, before being relaunched in its own name.

The town's supermarket has seen several re-brandings. The first to claim the name – advertising 'Wincanton has a supermarket!' in 1984 – was the Spar Foodliner in the High Street. The second location, in Carrington Way, went from Gateway to Presto and then Safeway. The latter trading name was soon adopted by the parent company, Argyll Foods plc, as its own. Safeway then moved out of town, to a 'superstore' beside a new roundabout within sight of the A303, and was taken over by Sir Ken Morrison in 2004.

Discussions on the route for the last stage of the dual carriageway that now carries the A303 from Sparkford to Mere began on the afternoon of 15 May

Opened in 1856, the Police Station looked just the same on closure in 1971, facing the entrance to St Joseph's (foreground) before the building of Waterside estate on the other side of the wall (left).

Embarkation leave for Bob Meatyard (centre right) in Richmond Place, Silver Street, as he parted from his motorcycle and friends and family, including Monty Eddington (left), Jean Meatyard (centre) and Peter Coffin (right).

MODERN WINCANTON

Gathering on the site of Acorn House for an open-air service to mark the start of construction work on the twin towers of the Priory Church, in South Street, in 1907.

Right: *The wedding of Antony Graziano and Jane Hamblin, in the Catholic Church in 2003.*

Bishop Ambrose Burton, from Clifton Cathedral, laid the foundation-stone of St Luke's Priory Church on 7 November 1907.

Carmelite Priory (right) *and Catholic Church of St Luke and St Teresa* (left), *in 2002, shortly before their lawns became a building site.*

Southern view of the Catholic Church and its outbuildings in 2000.

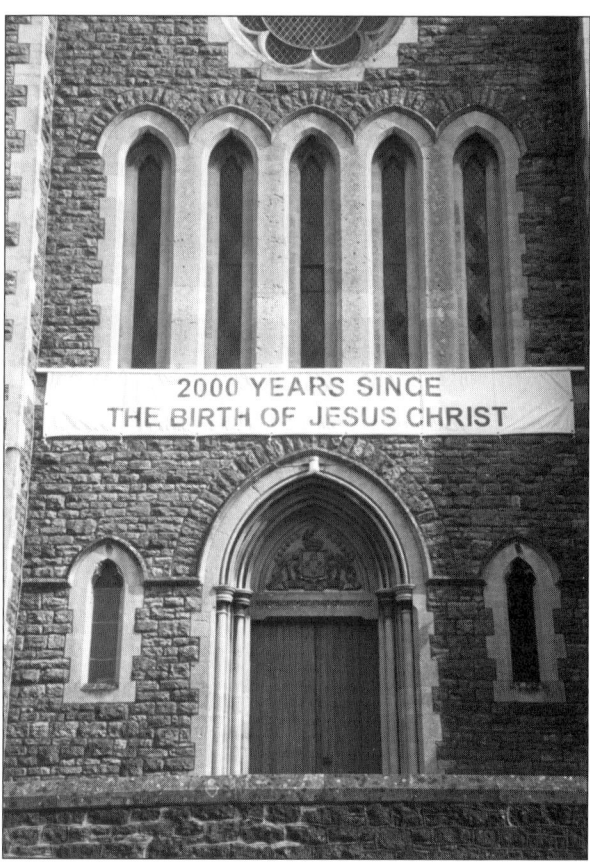

Millennium message over the main door of the Catholic Church in 2000.

1986 after the Department of the Environment had announced its plans. The main impact was to cut apart a strip of superb orchid marsh and old orchard at Leigh Common, southwards from Hunter's Lodge Inn to Beech Lane, which was the only registered common land in the vicinity of Wincanton. Rob Jarman and Dave Reid of Somerset Trust for Nature Conservation gathered the various interested parties into what became a public meeting in the middle of Hunter's Lodge car park. They outlined the significance of the threatened 9 acres to a gathering that included representatives of South Somerset District Council, the Countryside Commission, three local parishes, and the Open Spaces Society. I was the latter spokesman. The parishes were represented by Mrs Allard and Mr Trott of Stoke Trister, Alan Osbourne from Charlton Musgrove, and David Ford from Penselwood. There were also some farmers whose land would be affected by the roadworks.

'Put the road through the common, that's the best place for it,' one of them told us. 'It hasn't been used for anything for years.' Another local resident, from Stoke Trister, took the district council official to task for claiming that it maintained a bridleway southwards to the village: 'It is impassable. The old Wincanton council used to send two or three men along to clear it but it hasn't been touched for more than 20 years. No one uses it.'

This side issue had generated considerable controversy because the Environment Department was proposing to spend some £60,000 on a bridge to carry the unusable bridleway across the new dual carriageway. Yet Beech Lane, from Stoke Trister to Leigh Common, was earmarked for closure. 'You can see his point,' the man from the Countryside Commission conceded.

We then heard that the Environment Department was going to find some 'exchange land' in compensation for bulldozing Leigh Common. Possible replacement ground, being a steep slope with a copse running down to a stream, was then inspected by the group. There were questions about the legal status of alternative land. As the representative of the Open Spaces Society I explained that it would carry the same grazing rights and responsibilities – plus eventual public access – as the land it replaced. One or two people were fussed that the existing common lay in Stoke Trister whereas some land we had seen was in the southern extremity of the parish of Penselwood. I tried to reassure them that this made no difference as common land frequently spreads across parish boundaries and can in fact be held in common by qualifying residents of more than one parish. It already carried the right – unexercised for years – for the tethering of a token cow from Penselwood.

Stoke Trister folk seemed to think the common belonged to them but the district council man said no one had turned up at an ownership hearing in 1967. He assumed the historic owners were the Phelips family as lords of the manor. Such doubts are the norm with common land and matter not a jot.

Our first surprise, earlier in the day, was that the two oaks on the edge of this proposed alternative land, immediately east of the Stoke Trister turning, were now lying as logs on the ground. 'That's my first job in the morning,' Rob Jarman told us, 'to get a TPO (tree preservation order) put on that ash down there and the trees in the copse.' The sceond surprise was the view. Whereas Leigh Common had a vista entirely filled by the A303 and its almost continuous traffic, this field looked the other way – southwards – across the valley of the Cale and into the Blackmore Vale, to hills beyond Templecombe and Stalbridge.

Floristically, as well as scenically, the land began to raise expectations. There was a drift of cowslips. Chesils Copse, at the top of the valley, displayed a floor smothered with ransoms, the flowers of wild garlic, interspersed with mare's tails, marsh marigolds, bluebells and ferns. The ground became spongy and was obviously on the spring line. That then provided our next surprise. It gushed from the hillside as a torrent.

If there was a more general surprise it was that the alternative land, being on a slope facing away from the road, had none of the incessant sound of main road traffic that we found so overpowering on Leigh Common. It was a peaceful interlude until we arrived back at the felled oaks and encountered the farmer, young R.W.G. Foot from Encie Farm which is on the north side of the Gillingham turning, who was unaware of the site visit. I assumed the role of apologist for the group and tried to explain that we were there for the quasi-legal purpose of formulating some considered advice for the Secretary of State for the Environment, in my case because he asks the Open Spaces Society for our opinion of development proposals that affect common land.

Most of us held files of papers and maps but no one noticed the fact that we had not entered his land as trespassers. The gate we had used was on a public footpath, south-eastwards to Clapton Farm, but a courtesy call to Encie Farm would have been polite. Back in the comparative tranquillity of the car park at Hunter's Lodge, Richard Bull summed up the general feeling about the proposals, in which we effectively agreed to move the common.

In the town centre in 1987, the old premises of Sarum Furnishing on the south side of the High Street was converted into Applegarth shopping mall, by Pam and Peter Bridgwood. It was named by Pam Bridgwood for Merlin's residence 'to the east of Camelot' (Cadbury Castle) in Mary Stewart's series of novels based on the Arthurian legends. Roy Sansom retired on Christmas Eve that year, to Dancing Lane, after half a century as a 'traditional gentleman's barber'. He had started with Jack Masters in a room above Harry Case's fish shop in

Above: *Post Office staff outside their office in No. 20 High Street* (left) *in about 1895.*

Left: *The insignia of George V on a motorcycle sidecar making a country house delivery from Wincanton in 1921.*

Miss Eliza Ings, the town's postmistress in 1890, with her all-male staff. Two display Empire campaign medals.

MODERN WINCANTON

Charles William Tolley, Wincanton's postmaster in 1911 (left of the ladies) with his staff, of whom at least two are wearing military medals.

Almost empty boxes (right) in the postal sorting office at No. 20 High Street on its closure in 1974.

Postwar offices of solicitors Dyne, Hughes and Archer (left), and a Royal Mail collection from Wincanton Post Office in its location since 1974, as observed from the roof of No. 7 Market Place in 1991.

The new Elizabethan age was marked with the biggest celebration since Queen Victoria's diamond jubilee.

The River Cale (foreground), Hook Field (left) and Cemetery Lane (centre) – planted with an avenue of trees in 1888 – looking northwards to West Hill in 1905.

the Market Place, in January 1937. In 1949 he took over the business and then moved it around the corner, to a shop in South Street, in 1957.

Private sheltered housing provision came to Wincanton in 1987 with the building of Homecanton House in Carrington Way by Hampshire developers McCarthy and Stone. Proclaiming the virtues of the rural idyll for 'a home for life', regional manager Bernard Land became somewhat carried away by his own brochures and referred to the location as 'the charming village of Wincanton'. He was also taken to task for 'the clumsy Homecanton name' and explained that his firm always started with the word 'Home' and added 'an appropriate local suffix'.

The Waterside estate was built across an old orchard on the west side of North Street in 1988. The refurbished Town Hall was opened by the former editor of *The Times*, William Rees-Mogg, on 2 November 1991 after lunch with Brigadier Peter Newth and a visit to his ancestral home at the Dogs, courtesy of owner Dr Samir Mattar.

After various issues had been resolved, by the end of the decade, the section of the old A303 eastwards from Bayford, through Bourton and Zeals, was replaced by a dual carriageway in 1991. Wimpey were the main contractors. 'Major Roads Works for 3 Miles,' their signs read.

Leigh Common still exists, as a roadside strip of orchids and old apple trees facing Hunter's Lodge Inn, and the exchange land eventually obtained – currently being mapped by the Countryside Agency as 'open country' with public access – lies to the south-east. It is on the other side of the dual carriageway, either side of the top end of the public path that drops down towards Clapton Farm, and includes much of what I saw on the site visit.

A century of latter-day monasticism in Wincanton ended in May 1995 with the closure of the Carmelite Priory and secondment of its last priests to a mission for Nigeria. The Nigerians, on welcoming them, predicted that they would soon be sending missionaries to Britain.

These days, a substantial proportion of the glossy bumf that comes through the letter-box has been printed in Wincanton, although it seldom carries the name of the Wincanton Print Company. They are print farmers, acting as subcontractors and working anonymously around the clock for other printers and advertising agencies, having doubled in size twice since moving from the National School to purpose-built premises in Wessex Way. Steve Taylor added offices, in 2002, that brought the first flourish of characterful architecture to Wincanton Business Park. Although the frontage has a 1930s-style curve, with plenty of glass, the basic building is in golden Hamstone. It was finished off with a grotesque medieval corbel stone which I found in rubble from the ruins of Montacute Abbey.

Rising above the town, under a great domed roof, King Arthur's Community School now boasts a competition-sized swimming-pool. Out of town in the other direction, down in Moor Lane, Wincanton Sports Ground brought the town's general facilities into the new millennium beside the Maddocks Pavilion, in the shape and size of an aircraft hangar.

My parochial campaigns over the years have resulted in two minor successes. It took 15 years to get signs erected to the Racecourse. Before that, if I ventured into the street at lunchtime on Thursdays in its calendar, I would spend half an hour directing

MODERN WINCANTON

The class of '75, being the top year at Wincanton Primary School, mostly still living in the town and celebrating their 40th birthdays in 2005.

traffic. The other achievement, after tipping over yet another trolley of Whiskas on kerbstones beside the town's first supermarket – to roll down the slope into Carrington Way – was to persuade Argyll Foods to provide a ramp across the obstacle.

Such measures used to be big news in a small town. 'Wake up Wincanton!' I once wrote. Now, however, I'm quite relieved when it goes back to sleep. The town becomes particularly dream-like when characters descend upon it from the pages of the *Discworld* series of novels by Wiltshire author Terry Pratchett. Born on 28 April 1948, and schooled in public relations as the press officer for the pre-privatisation Central Electricity Generating Board, he escaped into another world of fame and fortune by 'letting the mind wander'. Real-life Wincanton is twinned with his fictional town of Ankh-Morpork.

Devotees will know how they handle the planning process there. Here, Wincanton has been advancing up West Hill for the past three decades. The latest 'consultation masterplan' from South Somerset District Council, published in 2005, is set to take the town's population to more than 6,000 by filling the last green gap in the urban jigsaw.

Abbey Manor Homes are prepared to build 250 dwellings between the industrial estate at Dyke's Way and the junction with Dancing Lane at the top of the hill. The remainder of the 30-acre site east of New Barns is earmarked for a new primary school, an extension to the churchyard, and slivers of open space and what is termed 'strategic landscape'. Its file code for officialdom is KS/WINC/1 which stands for Wincanton Key Site No. 1. The bigger controversy for the future will be where next for project No. 2? I shall make that a rhetorical question mark.

Exercise time for the mallards, in a view westwards across a spongy recreation-ground towards the cemetery in 2004.

143

Above: *Cherry blossom time in the recreation-ground, looking southwards from the bridge to the bandstand (top right), in 2004.*

Left: *Pollarded lime tree and a sign of the times, banning outdoor drinking of alcohol, in 2004.*

Cemetery Lane and pollarded limes planted in 1888, looking eastwards in 2004, between the back gardens of Rickhayes (left) *and the recreation-ground* (right).

MODERN WINCANTON

Above: *Lych-gate at the churchyard looking suitably sombre on a wet day in 2004.*

Right: *The centre of the cemetery, with the grave of a wartime airman* (centre foreground) *between those of John Samuel Harrop Bingham and William Besant.*

Below: *Northwards from the cemetery to the roofs of Victorian villas from the Mount* (top left) *to West Hill House* (top right) *in 2004.*

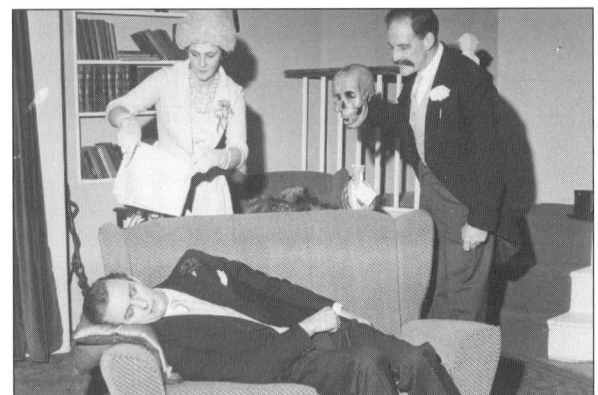

Above: *Philip Felstead (seated right) starred in the political comedy 'The Manor of Northstead' performed by Wincanton Players in 1971.*

Left: *Cathy Rhodes with Peter Hutchings (right) and a body, in 'Bridle Bachelor' from the spring of 1965.*

Below: *'Quiet Weekend' in May 1963, included among others: Monty Carswell (left), Peter Hutchings, Mrs Dyke, Mrs Banks, Graham Dyke, Mrs Scammell, Dennis Rays.*

MODERN WINCANTON

Above: *The weir on the River Cale, beside Shatterwell House, in January 1963.*

Right: *Shatterwell House* (left) *and No. 8 Shatterwell Cottages* (right) *with hoar frost on the trees of Cash's Park* (centre), *in an old-style winter's day in the 1990s.*

Below: *Bridge over the River Cale, at Burton's Mill Farm in January 1963, which fell to another natural event – being washed away in June 1982.*

Above: *Derek Roberts of Mears Construction Ltd* (centre), *with David Cave* (right) *representing the town, preparing to cut the ribbon and open Wincanton bypass in March 1977.*

Left: *Eastwards from Lawrence Hill, towards Wincanton* (left) *and Stoke Trister* (centre), *from the Exeter-bound lane of the A303 in February 1978.*

Royal Navy Wasp on display in the Safeway car park for the Xray Tango Helicopter Club in 2002.

MODERN WINCANTON

Above and right: *Wincanton Sports Ground, in Moor Lane, and its new Maddocks Pavilion in 2001.*

Below: *Desert Orchid, Britain's favourite racehorse, returning in retirement during 1991. Wincanton was the scene of many of his triumphs.*

149

THE BOOK OF WINCANTON

Above: *High Street stalls between the Green Dragon (left)* and *Gourmet House (right), during the Wincanton Festival in 2002.*

Left: *Prizewinners collecting their envelopes from Sir Cameron Mackintosh (left).*

Below: *Christine Dean and Sir Cameron Mackintosh (left), the theatre impresario who owns Stavordale Priory, with the town crier in front of Uncle Tom's Cabin.*

MODERN WINCANTON

Above: *The town crier leading festival organiser Christine Dean, guest Sir Cameron Mackintosh and mayor Frank Foster, up the High Street in 2002.*

Right: *Face paint with the young lady's Union Flag being for Queen Elizabeth II's golden jubilee in 2002.*

Below: *Organisers of the Wincanton Festival gathering at the Balsam Centre.*

THE BOOK OF WINCANTON

Top: *The bus of the Royal British Legion and stalls blocking the High Street during the Wincanton Festival in 2002.*

Mayor Frank Foster (top) and impresario Sir Cameron Mackintosh giving out fancy-dress prizes at the Wincanton Festival in 2002.

Above: *Bell-ringers performing in the High Street.*

Pearly princesses with golden jubilee flags for Queen Elizabeth II at a fancy-dress contest in the grounds of the Balsam Centre.

MODERN WINCANTON

Church View Court, opposite the churchyard on the site of a garage in Station Road, on completion in 2002.

Former Typewriter Shop and yard of builders Holt and Masters awaiting redevelopment in 2004.

Redevelopment, in kit form, by Bill Hopkins of the west side of North Street between the Market Place and the National School over the winter of 2004–05.

Flats and apartments taking shape behind the North Street scaffolding.

MODERN WINCANTON

'Wincanton, Grande Bretagne' on the road sign for twin town Gennes et Les Rosiers in France.

Wincanton is the Ankh-Morpork of Terry Pratchett's Discworld *novels, whose residents gathered around the Memorial Hall in 2002.*

THE BOOK OF WINCANTON

Above: *Author Terry Pratchett* (right) *and bodyguard.*

Left and below: *Characters from the pages of* Discworld *reviewed in the Memorial Hall in 2002.*

Subscribers

Susan J. Adams (née Whitmarsh), Yeovil, Somerset
Ron, Peggy and Roger Allen, Butlers Fish Shop
Phillip John Andrews, Wincanton, Somerset
D.J. and S.L. Bain, Wincanton, Somerset
Michael and Elisabeth Balfour
J. Barr, Taunton, Somerset
Samuel J. Bartlett, Wincanton, Somerset
Ms L. Batchelor, Wincanton
Ken Bennett, Wincanton
John Blake, Wincanton, Somerset
Sue Boulton and Steve Bain, Wincanton, Somerset
Mrs Joan Bowie, Wincanton
Gerald and Barbara Box
The Bundy's, Wincanton, Somerset
Arthur G. Butler, Wincanton, Somerset
Lesley Butt, Wincanton
Mrs E. Cameron (née Hayter), Berinsfield, Oxon
Christine Carron, Wincanton, Somerset
John David Chilcott, Stoketrister, Somerset
B.J. Coombes, Wincanton, Somerset
Colin and Angela Cornwell, Sedgehill, Dorset
Frederick W. Cox, North Mymms, Hertfordshire
Mr James Crocker, Wincanton, Somerset
Richard and Gill D'Arcy, Wincanton, Somerset
Michael Dixon, Stoke Trister, Somerset
Francis Dukes, Penselwood, Somerset
Rebecca R. Eastment, Wincanton, Somerset
Judith and John Ellingham, Charlton Musgrove
Nigel and Rosemary Engert
Sarah Faithfull, Horsington, Somerset
Dr M.J. Fellows, Wincanton
Christopher and Jane Fenton, Wincanton, Somerset
Gordon and Stella Ford
Mr B. Fry, Wincanton, Somerset

M.B. de C. Giles M.R.C.V.S., Bayford, Somerset
Ken and Dee Gosling, North Cheriton, Somerset
Mike and Rose Gray, Holton, Somerset
Andrew J. Green, Cradlehall, Inverness
John M. Green, Lochardil, Inverness
Thomas E. Green, Wincanton, Somerset
Mervyn Gulliford, Wincanton, Somerset
A.A. Haines, Martock
R.P. Hawes, Wincanton, Somerset
Mr and Mrs Keven and Sandra Hawkins, Wincanton, Somerset
Iris Heald (Perrett), Wincanton
Mollie and Michael Holmes, Balsam Fields, Wincanton
Len Holt, Wincanton, Somerset
Georgina Hopkins, Verrington Farm, Wincanton
Nathan W. Hopkins, Wincanton
N.W. Hopkins, Furzewood, Suddon, Wincanton
W.I. Hopkins, Wincanton, Somerset
Robert J. Humphries, Wincanton, Somerset
Derek Hurst, Gillingham
P.W.E. Judd, North Cheriton, Somerset
R.K. Judd, Shaftesbury, Dorset
Mr and Mrs Judges, Wincanton, Somerset
Bob and Finn Kennedy, Preview, Wincanton
B. Kiddle, Bayford
Edwin and Maureen Kiddle, Bayford
Lorraine King, Wincanton, Somerset
The Kirkby Family, South Street, Wincanton, Somerset
Vivien Larcombe, Wincanton, Somerset
Hannah L. Lee, Wincanton
Charles C. Lethbridge
Jo and Gary Lipthorpe-Nye, Wincanton
Colin R. Mahoney, Wincanton, Somerset
Emma Marks, Wincanton, Somerset
Gillian McCarthy, The Stop Gap, Shepton Montague

Murray and Serena McLaren
Audrey I. Meade, Burrowbridge, Somerset
Denis and Mary Miller, Shaftesbury, Dorset
Mrs F. Mills, Wincanton, Somerset
Mrs D.M. Morrison, Wincanton
Mr Brian Nash, Wincanton
Jim and Pauline O'Gorman, Maperton
Alan Osborne, Bayford, Wincanton
Morley J. Parker, Wincanton, Somerset
David Perrett, Wincanton, Somerset
Adrian and Joan Phillips, Wincanton
Ann and Bryan Phillips, Wincanton
Constance Poole
Mike and Corinne Porter, The Old Police Station, Wincanton
P. and T. Raymond, Belgium
Michael G. Rendell, Wincanton
E.M. Rochford, Wincanton, Somerset
Fenton Rutter
Jonathan and Tristan Sams, Wincanton
Michael and Doreen Shave and Family, Wincanton, Somerset
Robert A. Shave
Frances M. Sheldrake, Wincanton
Pat and Terry Sheppard, Wincanton
Aubrey F. Short, Wincanton, Somerset
Mrs P. Shutler (née Lucas), born 23.12.13.
Gordon and Tricia Smith, Wincanton, Somerset
Helen and Derek Smith, Wincanton, Somerset
Gerald and Mary Anne Stephenson, Wincanton, Somerset
Mike Stevens, Cucklington, Wincanton, Somerset

Norman Stone, Wincanton
Rich Stump, RAM Sports, Wincanton
Cheryl and Donald Tanner, Beech Tree Cottage, Wincanton
Mrs J. Thompson, Penselwood, Somerset
J. Todd, Wincanton, Somerset
Winifred Mary Trotter, Shepton Montague
Brian Tufton, Wincanton
Sarah Tufton, Wincanton
Jennifer S. Tume, Wincanton, Somerset
Richard D. Vincent, Wincanton, Somerset
Ian Wainwright, The Bear Inn, Wincanton
Vera and Jack (John) Wake, Wincanton
C.G. Waldron, Coat
John F.W. Walling, Newton Abbot, Devon
Michael A. Watts, Wincanton, Somerset
Mike and Rosie Wheeler, Stoke Trister
Mr David and Kim White, Mere, Wiltshire
Mrs Helen White, Wincanton, Somerset
Mrs Karen Virginia White, Wincanton, Somerset
Ken and Marion White, Wincanton, Somerset
Michael J. White, Wincanton, Somerset
Mr Robert and Mrs Wendy White, Aldershot, Hampshire
The White Horse Hotel, Wincanton
Patricia J. Whitmarsh, Wincanton, Somerset
Graham J. Wilkins, Henstridge, Somerset
Wincanton Primary School
Thelma J. Wiscombe, Wincanton, Somerset
Norman J. Woof, Wincanton
Joan and David Wright, Wincanton, Somerset

FURTHER TITLES

Community Histories

The Book of Addiscombe • Canning and Clyde Road Residents Association and Friends
The Book of Addiscombe, Vol. II • Canning and Clyde Road Residents Association and Friends
The Book of Ashburton • Stuart Hands and Pete Webb
The Book of Axminster with Kilmington • Les Berry and Gerald Gosling
The Book of Bakewell • Trevor Brighton
The Book of Bampton • Caroline Seward
The Book of Barnstaple • Avril Stone
The Book of Barnstaple, Vol. II • Avril Stone
The Book of The Bedwyns • Bedwyn History Society
The Book of Bergh Apton • Geoffrey I. Kelly
The Book of Bickington • Stuart Hands
The Book of Bideford • Peter Christie and Alison Grant
Blandford Forum: A Millennium Portrait • Blandford Forum Town Council
The Book of Boscastle • Rod and Anne Knight
The Book of Bourton-on-the-Hill, Batsford and Sezincote • Allen Firth
The Book of Bramford • Bramford Local History Group
The Book of Breage & Germoe • Stephen Polglase
The Book of Bridestowe • D. Richard Cann
The Book of Bridport • Rodney Legg
The Book of Brixham • Frank Pearce
The Book of Buckfastleigh • Sandra Coleman
The Book of Buckland Monachorum & Yelverton • Pauline Hamilton-Leggett
The Book of Budleigh Salterton • D. Richard Cann
The Book of Carharrack • Carharrack Old Cornwall Society
The Book of Carshalton • Stella Wilks and Gordon Rookledge
The Parish Book of Cerne Abbas • Vivian and Patricia Vale
The Book of Chagford • Iain Rice
The Book of Chapel-en-le-Frith • Mike Smith
The Book of Chittlehamholt with Warkleigh & Satterleigh • Richard Lethbridge
The Book of Chittlehampton • Various
The Book of Codford • Romy Wyeth
The Book of Colney Heath • Bryan Lilley
The Book of Constantine • Moore and Trethowan
The Book of Cornwood and Lutton • Compiled by the People of the Parish

The Book of Crediton • John Heal
The Book of Creech St Michael • June Small
The Book of Crowcombe, Bicknoller and Sampford Brett • Maurice and Joyce Chidgey
The Book of Crudwell • Tony Pain
The Book of Cullompton • Compiled by the People of the Parish
The Book of Dawlish • Frank Pearce
The Book of Dulverton, Brushford, Bury & Exebridge • Dulverton and District Civic Society
The Book of Dunster • Hilary Binding
The Book of Easton • Easton Village History Project
The Book of Edale • Gordon Miller
The Ellacombe Book • Sydney R. Langmead
The Book of Exmouth • W.H. Pascoe
The Book of Grampound with Creed • Bane and Oliver
The Book of Gosport • Lesley Burton and Brian Musselwhite
The Book of Haughley • Howard Stephens
The Book of Hayle • Harry Pascoe
The Book of Hayling Island & Langstone • Peter Rogers
The Book of Helston • Jenkin with Carter
The Book of Hemyock • Clist and Dracott
The Book of Herne Hill • Patricia Jenkyns
The Book of Hethersett • Hethersett Society Research Group
The Book of High Bickington • Avril Stone
The Book of Honiton • Gerald Gosling
The Book of Ilsington • Dick Wills
The Book of Kingskerswell • Carsewella Local History Group
The Book of Lamerton • Ann Cole and Friends
Lanner, A Cornish Mining Parish • Sharron Schwartz and Roger Parker
The Book of Leigh & Bransford • Malcolm Scott
The Second Book of Leigh & Bransford • Malcolm Scott
The Book of Litcham with Lexham & Mileham • Litcham Historical and Amenity Society
The Book of Llangain • Haydyn Williams
The Book of Loddiswell • Loddiswell Parish History Group
The New Book of Lostwithiel • Barbara Fraser
The Book of Lulworth • Rodney Legg
The Book of Lustleigh • Joe Crowdy
The Book of Lydford • Compiled by Barbara Weeks
The Book of Lyme Regis • Rodney Legg
The Book of Manaton • Compiled by the People of the Parish

THE BOOK OF WINCANTON

The Book of Markyate • Markyate Local History Society
The Book of Mawnan • Mawnan Local History Group
The Book of Meavy • Pauline Hemery
The Book of Mere • Dr David Longbourne
The Book of Minehead with Alcombe • Binding and Stevens
The Book of Monks Orchard and Eden Park • Ian Muir and Pat Manning
The Book of Morchard Bishop • Jeff Kingaby
The Book of Mylor • Mylor Local History Group
The Book of Narborough • Narborough Local History Society
The Book of Newdigate • John Callcut
The Book of Newtown • Keir Foss
The Book of Nidderdale • Nidderdale Museum Society
The Book of Northlew with Ashbury • Northlew History Group
The Book of North Newton • J.C. and K.C. Robins
The Book of North Tawton • Baker, Hoare and Shields
The Book of Nynehead • Nynehead & District History Society
The Book of Okehampton • Roy and Ursula Radford
The Book of Ottery St Mary • Gerald Gosling and Peter Harris
The Book of Paignton • Frank Pearce
The Book of Penge, Anerley & Crystal Palace • Peter Abbott
The Book of Peter Tavy with Cudlipptown • Peter Tavy Heritage Group
The Book of Pimperne • Jean Coull
The Book of Plymtree • Tony Eames
The Book of Poole • Rodney Legg
The Book of Porlock • Dennis Corner
Postbridge – The Heart of Dartmoor • Reg Bellamy
The Book of Priddy • Albert Thompson
The Book of Princetown • Dr Gardner-Thorpe
The Book of Probus • Alan Kent and Danny Merrifield
The Book of Rattery • By the People of the Parish
The Book of Roadwater, Leighland and Treborough • Clare and Glyn Court
The Book of St Austell • Peter Hancock
The Book of St Day • Joseph Mills and Paul Annear
The Book of St Dennis and Goss Moor • Kenneth Rickard
The Book of St Levan • St Levan Local History Group
The Book of Sampford Courtenay with Honeychurch • Stephanie Pouya
The Book of Sculthorpe • Gary Windeler

The Book of Seaton • Ted Gosling
The Book of Sidmouth • Ted Gosling and Sheila Luxton
The Book of Silverton • Silverton Local History Society
The Book of South Molton • Jonathan Edmunds
The Book of South Stoke with Midford • Edited by Robert Parfitt
South Tawton & South Zeal with Sticklepath • Roy and Ursula Radford
The Book of Sparkwell with Hemerdon & Lee Mill • Pam James
The Book of Staverton • Pete Lavis
The Book of Stithians • Stithians Parish History Group
The Book of Stogumber, Monksilver, Nettlecombe & Elworthy • Maurice and Joyce Chidgey
The Book of South Brent • Greg Wall
The Book of Studland • Rodney Legg
The Book of Swanage • Rodney Legg
The Book of Tavistock • Gerry Woodcock
The Book of Thorley • Sylvia McDonald and Bill Hardy
The Book of Torbay • Frank Pearce
The Book of Truro • Christine Parnell
The Book of Uplyme • Gerald Gosling and Jack Thomas
The Book of Watchet • Compiled by David Banks
The Book of Wendling, Longham and Beeston with Bittering • Stephen Olley
The Book of West Huntspill • By the People of the Parish
The Book of Weston-super-Mare • Sharon Poole
The Book of Whitchurch • Gerry Woodcock
Widecombe-in-the-Moor • Stephen Woods
Widecombe – Uncle Tom Cobley & All • Stephen Woods
The Book of Williton • Michael Williams
The Book of Wincanton • Rodney Legg
The Book of Winscombe • Margaret Tucker
The Book of Witheridge • Peter and Freda Tout and John Usmar
The Book of Withycombe • Chris Boyles
Woodbury: The Twentieth Century Revisited • Roger Stokes
The Book of Woolmer Green • Compiled by the People of the Parish
The Book of Yetminster • Shelagh Hill

For details of any of the above titles or if you are interested in writing your own history, please contact: Commissioning Editor, Community Histories, Halsgrove House, Lower Moor Way, Tiverton, Devon EX16 6SS, England; email: katyc@halsgrove.com